DATE DUE

Copyright 2008	

PRINTED IN U.S.A.

Wyoming

WYOMING BY ROAD

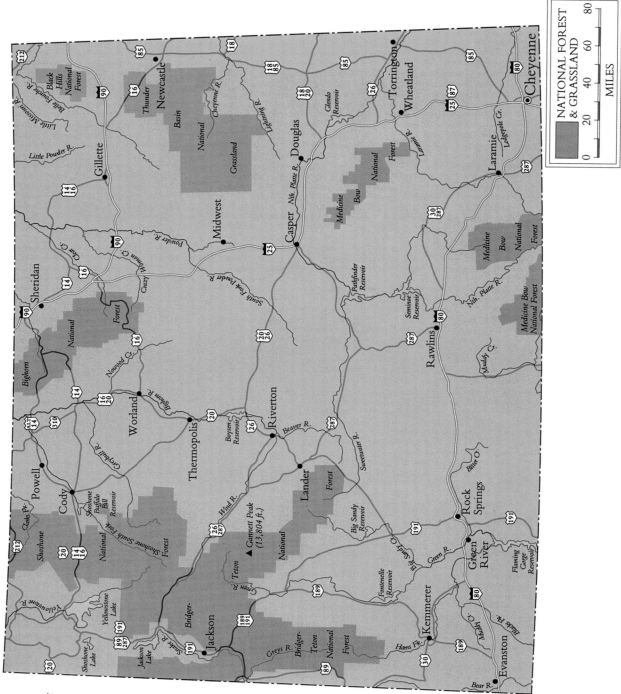

NATIONAL FOREST & GRASSLAND

MILES

0 20 40 60 80

Black Hills National Forest

Belle Fourche R.

Little Missouri R.

Little Powder R.

Gillette

Thunder Basin National Grassland

Newcastle

Cheyenne R.

Lightning R.

Douglas

Nth. Platte R.

Glendo Reservoir

Torrington

Wheatland

Cheyenne

Laramie

Lodgepole Cr.

Laramie R.

Medicine Bow National Forest

Midwest

Powder R.

Casper

Pathfinder Reservoir

Seminoe Reservoir

Nth. Platte R.

Medicine Bow National Forest

Sheridan

Clear Cr.

Crazy W.

South Fork Powder R.

Bighorn National Forest

Nowood Cr.

Worland

Bighorn R.

Riverton

Rawlins

Muddy Cr.

Powell

Cody

Shoshone National Forest

Buffalo Bill Reservoir

Shoshone

Clarks Fk.

Shoshone South Fork

Greybull R.

Thermopolis

Boysen Reservoir

Beaver R.

Lander

Forest

Sweetwater R.

Big Sandy Reservoir

Rock Springs

Green River

Flaming Gorge Reservoir

▲ Gannett Peak (13,804 ft.)

Wind R.

Teton

Green R.

Bridger-Teton National Forest

Big Sandy Cr.

Green R.

Fontenelle Reservoir

Kemmerer

Muddy Cr.

Blacks Fk.

Yellowstone R.

Yellowstone Lake

Jackson Lake

Shoshone Lake

Snake R.

Jackson

Bridger-Teton National Forest

Greys R.

Hams Fk.

Evanston

Bear R.

N E S W

Celebrate the States

Wyoming

Guy Baldwin and Joyce Hart

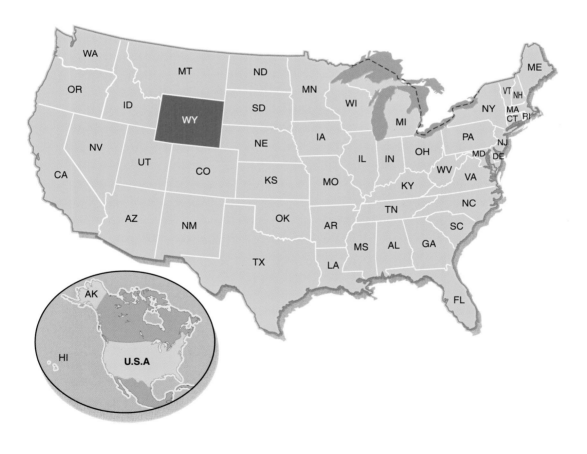

Marshall Cavendish
Benchmark
New York

Marshall Cavendish Benchmark
99 White Plains Road
Tarrytown, NY 10591-9001
www.marshallcavendish.us

All Internet addresses were correct and accurate at the time of printing.

Library of Congress Cataloging-in-Publication Data
Baldwin, Guy.
Wyoming / by Guy Baldwin and Joyce Hart. 2nd ed.
p. cm. (Celebrate the states)
Summary: "Provides comprehensive information on the geography, history, wildlife, governmental structure, economy, cultural diversity, peoples, religion, and landmarks of Wyoming"—Provided by publisher.
Includes bibliographical references and index.
ISBN 978-0-7614-2563-2
1. Wyoming—Juvenile literature. I. Hart, Joyce, 1954– II. Title.
F761.3.B35 2008
978.7dc22
2007019560

Editor: Christine Florie
Publisher: Michelle Bisson
Art Director: Anahid Hamparian
Series Designer: Adam Mietlowski

Photo research by Connie Gardner

Cover photo by LOOK Die Bildagentur der Fotografen GmbH/Alamy

The photographs in this book are used by permission and through the courtesy of: *Getty Images:* Joseph Van Os/Image Bank, back cover; Discovery Channel Images, 14; Altrendo, 17; Norbert Rosing/National Geographic, 24; Stringer/Time Life, 72, 131; Michael Melford, 84; Aurora, 94, 137; Getty Images Entertainment, 126; Arnold Newman Collection, 130; *Alamy:* BL Images Ltd., 8; Tom Tracy, 52; Holger Leve, 62, 108; Jim Harvey, 111; *Dembinsky Photo Associates:* Stan Osolinski, 19; *Bridgeman Art Library:* In The Teton Range, 1899 (oil on canvas), Moran, Thomas (1837-1926)/Private Collection, Photo Christie's Images; *North Wind Picture Archives:* 29, 30, 37, 40, 41, 44; *Art Resource:* Smithsonian American Art Museum, Washington, DC, 26; *The Granger Collection:* 33; *The Image Works:* US National Archives/Roger-Violett, 49; Andre Jenny, 98; Photri/Topham, 115 (T); *Gibson Stock Photography;* 56, 65, 105; *Photo Edit:* Mary Steinbacher, 58; Michelle D. Birdwell, 71; *SuperStock:* Richard Cummins, 74, 96; *AP Photo:* Ed Andrieski, 77; Gregory Hueing, 79, 80; *Corbis:* Joel W. Rogers, 11; Momatiuk-Eastcott, 12; Layne Kennedy, 15; Joe McDonald, 18; D. Roberts and Lorri Franz, 10, 115 (B); Darrell Gulin, 22; James L. Amos, 34, 124; Connie Ricca, 35; Franz Lanting, 47; CORBIS, 50, 132; Kevin R. Morris, 54, 101; Karl Weatherly, 60; Bob Krist, 63; Swift Vanuga Images, 68; Stefano Amantini, 86; Kevin Flemming, 188; Stephanie Maze, 89; George Steinmetz, 90; David Muench, 102; James Leynse, 103; Gunter Marx, 104; Buddy Mays, 112; Jeff Vanuga, 119; Reuters, 128; Craig Aurness, 135.

Printed in Malaysia
1 3 5 6 4 2

Contents

Wyoming Is . . .

. . . a land of secrets and surprises.

"So this was Wyoming, I thought, a secret, hidden world unknown to the rest of the country, serene and calm, with a slow heart beat."
—children's author Mary O'Hara

"The real secret of Wyoming's fascination is still basically *emptiness*. . . . Just to go along seeing nothing is a pleasure."
—writer Nathaniel Burt

People find Wyoming a great place to live.

"Wyoming is the friendliest state I have ever been in."
—journalist and author, John Gunther (from his book *Inside U.S.A.*)

"With a view of Pike's Peak to the left and Cheyenne, Wyoming, to the right, we really did have an idyllic upbringing in a post-card setting."
—actress Joan Van Ark

Wyoming is home to hard workers who enjoy making do.

"One year, the snow was so deep early in the month that Maurice couldn't get up to the Bighorns to cut our customary Christmas tree, and we found a huge tumbleweed, sprayed it with glitter and decorated it."
—author Betty Evenson

Wyoming is a land of strong individuals who love their state . . .

"Whether natives or immigrants, Wyomingites treat the state as a treasured resource. . . . Most of Wyoming's people enjoy a love affair with space."

—author Robert Harold Brown

"While there are certainly many things I love about Wyoming, I really enjoy our state's mountains and wide open spaces. I appreciate living where there are smaller, more people-oriented communities."

—U.S. Senator Craig Thomas (Wyoming)

. . . and who want to take care of it.

"I'm lucky to live in Cody, a small western town. . . . Nestled in the shadow of the Rocky Mountains, we enjoy big history, big mountains, big sky, and big wildlife. The breadth of the Western landscape is at our doorstep, reminding us how vital it is that we are a responsible caretaker of our heritage and environment."

—actor, author, and Buffalo Bill Art Show director Thom Huge

Wyoming remains a state of wide open spaces long after other western states have built up populous cities. The open space makes Wyomingites not only vigorously aware of the natural beauty of their state but also determined to protect it. Wyoming is a special place, peopled by special residents, who are more than proud to tell anyone who cares to know that they are from one of the most unique states in the Union.

Chapter One

A Rugged Wonderland

The shape of Wyoming (which measures 276 miles north to south and 364 miles east to west) is like a box filled with many treasures, including majestic grasslands, soaring mountains, sparkling lakes, and rushing rivers. Besides the wondrous geology of Yellowstone National Park, Flaming Gorge, and Devils Tower, there are swaying pine forests, severe desert basins, and a wide expanse of open lands. Wyoming is a land-locked state that shares its borders with Montana to the north and northwest, with South Dakota and Nebraska to the east, with Colorado to the south, with Utah to the southwest, and with Idaho to the west.

GRASSLANDS AND MOUNTAIN RANGES

Wyoming is best known for its amazing mountains, but it is also a Great Plains state, which means that it has its share of relatively flat grasslands. Much of eastern Wyoming is rolling grassland broken by rocky outcrops. This region resembles the neighboring areas of Montana, South Dakota, and Nebraska. The sky hangs like a blue tent over the land, and strong, steady

Wyoming's landscape includes lofty mountains and cool, running streams.

winds toss the grass in rippling waves. Cattle and sheep graze the plains, and most of Wyoming's farms are found here. There are few trees except along riverbanks. On most days, the clean, clear air allows people in eastern Wyoming to see for miles and miles.

South and west of the grasslands Wyoming rises up in awe-inspiring mountain ranges. The Laramie Mountains in the state's southeastern corner include peaks that are over 10,000 feet tall. Higher still are the Medicine Bow and Bighorn mountains in central Wyoming. The tallest mountains of all are farther west, especially in the northwest corner of the state, where the Absaroka and Teton ranges are found. The towering Grand Teton peak is 13,770 feet tall. But Wyoming's very highest mountain is Gannett Peak, which is located farther south, in the Wind River Mountains. It is 13,804 feet tall—more than 2.5 miles above sea level.

Although they are all part of the Rocky Mountains each of Wyoming's mountain ranges is different. Some are the result of one plate in the Earth's crust pushing another one up from below. This raises the upper plate and creates what are called uplifted mountains, such as the Medicine Bow Range. Others, such as the Tetons, rose up because of volcanic pressure below the Earth's surface. It is easy to see the difference between these two types of mountain formations. The layers of rock around uplifted ranges are tilted, so the mountains look like they were forced into the air from one side. The volcanic Tetons, by contrast, are shaped more like cones and push straight up into the sky.

In the state's northwest corner, not far from the Tetons, is one of the most spectacular natural areas in the United States: Yellowstone National Park. Yellowstone sits on what is referred to as a hot spot, where molten rock from the Earth's interior has been driven almost to the surface.

Adventurers cross a glacier on Wyoming's highest point, Gannett Peak.

The heat that this lava gives off produces hot springs, bubbling mudpots, and geysers—gushes of hot water that shoot into the air. Writer Rudyard Kipling was amazed by Yellowstone when he visited in 1910, calling it a "howling wilderness . . . full of all imaginable freaks of a fiery nature." Yellowstone serves as a refuge for many kinds of wildlife. It is one of the last places in the Lower 48 states where wild grizzly bears and bison can be found.

Wyoming's mountain ranges are dotted with lakes. The lakes are cold—usually too cold for swimming. The creeks and streams that carry water to the lakes are often cloudy, almost milky. This is

White, hot steam erupts from Clepsydra Geyser in Yellowstone National Park.

not pollution but rock dust, a mixture of minerals created by glaciers grinding away at the mountains. When these minerals settle in the mountain lakes, the result is astonishing hues of blue and green. These cloudy streams and brightly colored lakes actually contain some of the purest water in the United States.

LAND AND WATER

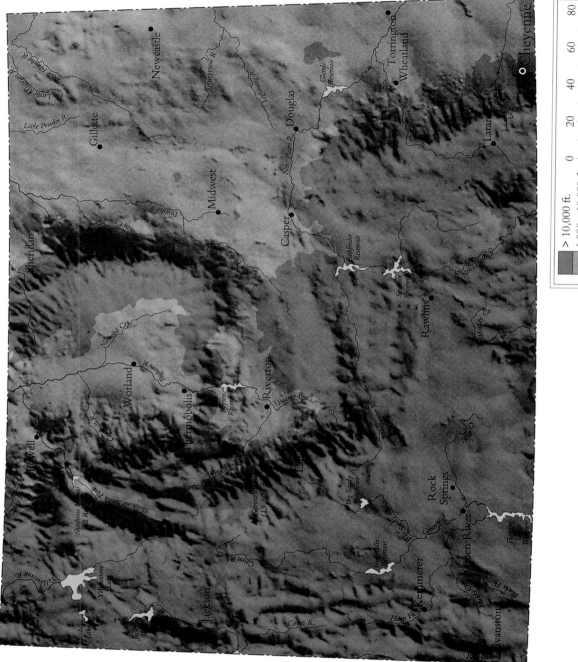

> 10,000 ft.

6,000 – 10,000 ft.

3,000 – 6,000 ft.

MILES

0   20   40   60   80

Newcastle

Gillette

Sheridan

Midwest

Douglas

Torrington
Wheatland

Laramie

Cheyenne

Casper

Pathfinder
Reservoir

Seminoe
Reservoir

Rawlins

Worland

Thermopolis

Riverton

Boysen
Reservoir

Rock
Springs

Green River

Kemmerer

Evanston

Jackson

Powell

Cody

Little Powder R.

Little Missouri R.

Belle Fourche R.

Cheyenne R.

Lightning R.

No. Platte R.

Glendo
Reservoir

Laramie R.

Powder R.

Clear Cr.

Tongue R.

No. Platte R.

Muddy Cr.

Bighorn R.

Norwood Cr.

Beaver R.

Sweetwater R.

Bitter Cr.

Bitter Cr.

Green R.

Green R.

Flaming
Gorge
Reservoir

Fontenelle
Reservoir

Big Sandy
Reservoir

Big Sandy R.

Wind R.

Popo Agie R.

Little R.

Shoshone R.

Greybull R.

Shoshone South Fork

Greys R.

Hams Fk.

Smiths Fk.

Black Fk.

Green R.

Yellowstone R.

Yellowstone
Lake

Jackson
Lake

N
E
S
W

WATER AND WEATHER

Between the mountain ranges are vast basins—bowl-like lowland areas. Water drains from the mountains and forms Wyoming's rivers. Some of these rivers spill into other rivers that eventually empty into the Pacific Ocean; others flow into a series of rivers leading to the Atlantic. The Continental Divide—the line separating water that drains into the Atlantic from rivers that are headed for the Pacific—zigzags through western Wyoming's highlands.

The Great Divide Basin, in south-central Wyoming, does not drain at all. If a lot of water accumulated there, it would become an enormous lake. But the basin gets only a few inches of rain each year and is among the country's driest areas. It is one of the few places in the United States with desert sand dunes.

The Killpecker Dunes are unique to Wyoming and, at 109,000 acres, are the largest active dune fields in North America.

PREHISTORIC LIFE IN WYOMING

Seventy-five million years ago the land that is now called Wyoming was underneath a great sea that covered much of what is now the American West. Lush swamps and forests thrived on the sea's edges, only to disappear beneath the water as the sea expanded. This process of the sea growing and then shrinking buried prehistoric life in layers of sediment that later hardened into rock, preserving fossils of Wyoming's earliest inhabitants. Scientists have recovered the remains of rhinoceroses, monkeys, crocodiles, cheetahs, and rabbit-sized horses in Wyoming. They have also found palm trees, roses, ferns, and many other ancestors of present-day plant life.

Most stunning, perhaps, are the dinosaur fossils that lie buried all across the state. Wyoming was once home to the triceratops, the stegosaurus, the huge apatosaurus, and the fierce tyrannosaurus.

Important fossils found in Wyoming are displayed in science museums. At Fossil Butte National Monument, near Kemmerer, visitors can even watch modern-day scientists dig up newly found fossils.

Several of Wyoming's rivers have carved majestic canyons. The Grand Canyon of the Yellowstone River is the most spectacular, with cliffs as high as 1,200 feet. The river cascades down two splendid waterfalls in Yellowstone Park. At the Lower Falls, the river plunges 308 feet (nearly twice as far as Niagara Falls in New York and Canada).

When they are not streaming through canyons, Wyoming's creeks and rivers have a characteristic look to them. They are fast, shallow, and muddy. Their size changes dramatically with the seasons. In the spring and early summer Wyoming's rivers are swollen with melted snow, but by late summer the waterways can shrink to just a trickle or dry up altogether. This is because of Wyoming's dry climate.

In Wyoming the average yearly rainfall is only 14.5 inches, but this number varies across the state. In parts of some mountain ranges as much as 50 inches of rain can fall in one year.

The low rate of precipitation, added to the state's high altitude, makes much of the state cool, even in the summer. Yellowstone's average July temperature is only 59 degrees Fahrenheit. However, the mean summer temperature for the state falls somewhere between 70 degrees and 80 degrees. In the highlands, the temperature can fall below freezing any month of the year. Over the course of the day the temperature can also change a great deal. Nights are chilly, but afternoons are often warm during the summer in most parts of the state. People learn to wear several layers of clothing, pulling layers off as needed. The warmest parts of the state are found in the Big Horn Basin, the lower elevations, and along the eastern border. The all-time hottest temperature of 14 degrees was recorded in 1900 in the town of Basin. In 1933 Grand Teton National Park captured the record for the coldest temperature, which was –66 degrees.

The Lower Falls in Yellowstone National Park formed about 590,000 years ago as a result of volcanic eruptions and lava flow.

The long, frigid winters can seem to last forever. High winds and low temperatures produce a dangerous windchill. Even a few minutes outdoors without proper clothing can lead to frostbite. Snow might only dust the grasslands and western basins, but in the mountains, snow falls by the truckload. At some places in the Tetons snowfall averages 176 inches, and in Yellowstone snowfall averages 150 inches.

The thick coat of a bison helps ward off the frigid temperatures of a Wyoming winter.

PLANTS AND ANIMALS

The incredible diversity of Wyoming's landscape has made it home to an equally diverse collection of plants and animals. Few states contain such a variety of wildlife: 119 species of mammals, 371 species of birds, and 9 species of snakes. The lakes and rivers contain a large assortment of fish, including salmon, bass, catfish, and seven kinds of trout. White pelicans and trumpeter swans soar over the lakes, as do peregrine falcons and ospreys.

Most of the nation's large mammals can be found in Wyoming. Moose and elk range across much of the state, living in the mountains during the summer and foraging in the valleys in the winter. The largest remaining herds of bighorn sheep live here, too. They descend from the Wind River Mountains to the foothills every winter to graze and mate. Everywhere, but especially on the eastern plains, white-tailed deer and the swift pronghorn antelope thrive.

The largest herd of big horn sheep in North America can be found in the Whiskey Mountain region of Wyoming.

PRONGHORNS

If there were a footrace for all the animals in North America, the winner would be the pronghorn antelope, which can reach speeds of more than 60 miles an hour.

More pronghorns live in Wyoming than anywhere else. They are timid creatures that usually move in groups, employing a "safety-in-numbers" approach to survival. Yet pronghorns have few fearsome predators in Wyoming (other than people). Why are they so fast and so cautious? One zoologist, John A. Byers, thinks that pronghorns developed these traits millions of years ago, when cheetahs, lions, and hyenas lived in Wyoming and preyed on the pronghorn. The last of these predators left the area about ten thousand years ago, but today's pronghorns act as though they were still present. It is as if the antelopes are "living with the ghosts" of their ancient enemies, Dr. Byers says.

The federal government owns almost half the land in Wyoming, including Grand Teton and Yellowstone national parks, five national forests, and several wildlife refuges. These places offer animals and plants homes where human development poses little threat. The Thunder Basin National Grassland in northeastern Wyoming helps preserve the more than 150 kinds of grass that are native to the state. The national forests sustain towering ponderosa and lodgepole pines and Douglas firs, an environment that is friendly to creatures such as squirrels, raccoons, pocket gophers, weasels, and wildcats. In several protected locations a few dozen of the world's last black-footed ferrets are struggling to rebuild their numbers. They are one of the most endangered mammals in North America.

Sixty-five million bison once lived in the American West, but they were hunted nearly to extinction in the nineteenth century. By 1905 a single ragged herd of twenty-five bison remained in Yellowstone Park. In 1997 there were approximately 3,500 Yellowstone bison—the largest herd in the world. But they are still in danger because some carry brucellosis, a disease that causes unborn calves to miscarry. This disease can spread to cattle, so when bison wander out of Yellowstone into Montana, officials in that state have them slaughtered to protect Montana's cattle industry. During the severe winter of 1997 many bison could not find enough food in Yellowstone. Some died of starvation; others headed for Montana to find grass and were killed. Half the Yellowstone herd was lost. Today, the herds have rebounded to between three thousand and four thousand animals.

LIVING WITH WILDLIFE

Laws protecting the state's animals and environment are supported by many Wyomingites. But ranchers and mining companies often oppose environmental programs that might limit their profits or their use of public land.

BISON—WYOMING'S STATE MAMMAL

Bison are truly majestic. Some are 6 feet tall from their hooves to their shoulders and weigh as much as 2,000 pounds. In 1985 the bison was named Wyoming's state mammal. In 2006 the number of bison at Yellowstone Park was still climbing, but so was the controversy concerning the transmission of the disease brucellosis. Cattle ranchers want bison to be vaccinated. Veterinarians question whether the vaccine is effective on bison. And animal rights activists are fighting to keep the bison vaccine-free and wild.

Glimpses of these shaggy animals can be seen at some of their favorite places to hang out, such as around the Mud Volcano area; along the Madison, Firehole, and Gibbons rivers; and at Hayden Valley, alongside the Yellowstone River.

In the past they usually got their way. Early in the century ranchers convinced the government to pay hunters to slaughter wolves that occasionally preyed on their livestock. By the 1920s the last of Wyoming's wolf packs had been exterminated.

In the early 1990s environmentalists proposed a plan to reintroduce wolves to Yellowstone National Park. Most ranchers fiercely opposed this idea, fearing that the wolves would leave the park to dine on their cattle and sheep. They came to public meetings carrying signs reading "Wyoming is Not a Zoo" and "Wolves Don't Pay Taxes." But others supported the wolves' return just as fiercely. "I know what it means to be an animal who doesn't know where to go, like the wolf and the grizzly bear," said Bill Tallbull, a Cheyenne Native American. "Now, I live on the reservation. It's my sanctuary. Let's let Yellowstone National Park be the sanctuary for the wolf."

Scientists predicted that the wolves would kill little livestock, and environmental organizations promised to pay ranchers if they did. Finally, a project was approved. In 1995 three wolf packs were captured in Canada and released in Yellowstone. Both sides of the conflict have followed the wolves' every move since then. Fortunately, the wolves are more interested in raising pups than in killing sheep. Their numbers are growing rapidly, and half of Wyomingites now support their return. The wolf packs are doing so well, as a matter of fact, that in 2007, the U.S. Fish and Wildlife Service began to discuss the possibility of taking wolves off the endangered list. This is both good news and bad news for the wolves. Delisting them means that wolves would be more threatened by hunters. Conservationist Rob Edward is concerned that taking wolves off the endangered list will rapidly deplete their numbers. "The nation's progress toward wolf recovery will grind to a halt under this plan," Edward said.

In May 2007, Wyoming's Game and Fish Department created a plan to "establish guide-lines for wolf management . . . while maintaining wolf/human contact."

On the other side of the issue are Wyoming's lawmakers, who, in 2007, passed a bill that delineated wolves as predators, paving the way to making the killing of wolves legal, even in national forest reserves. The debate continues.

Wolves are not the only endangered species in Wyoming. The Bureau of Land Management in Wyoming lists thirteen animals and four plants that are either threatened or endangered in the state. The plants include the butterfly plant, the blowout penstemon, the Ute ladies' tresses, and the desert yellowhead, which is found in central Wyoming, the only place on Earth where this plant still grows. Also on the endangered list are the grizzly bear, the whooping crane, the black-footed ferret, the lynx, and the Wyoming toad.

An advantage for most of Wyoming's wildlife is that the state's human population is tiny. Only about 515,000 people live in Wyoming, making it the least populated state in the country. There is an average of only five people per square mile (compared to an average of sixty-seven people per square mile for the whole United States).

Many Wyoming towns were originally built along major transportation routes. Not all cities were lucky enough to develop near important resources. Wyoming is scattered with ghost towns—communities that died out because there was little opportunity to prosper. In such places the sun beats down on rotting boards, and grass grows over the road. Abandoned buildings become homes for wild animals. Slowly the traces of settlement are swallowed up by the landscape, and once again the towering mountains and wide, empty spaces take over.

Chapter Two

High Country History

Groups of people may have lived in what is now Wyoming as early as 11,000 B.C.E., or more than 13,000 years ago. These groups include the Clovis (one of the earliest groups, who lived from about 13,000 years ago at the end of the last Ice Age), the Folsom (who lived from about 10,000 years ago), and the Plano (who lived from about 8,000 years ago).

Scientists do not know much about the earliest of these people, the Clovis, except that those who lived in this area moved frequently in search of food. They probably foraged for roots and seeds, and there is evidence that they also may have hunted large mammals such as the Ice Age mammoths. Tools made from the bones and tusks of animals have been excavated at archaeological sites, demonstrating the Clovis's hunting techniques. The Clovis were such successful hunters, one theory contends, that they might have overhunted the animals that were most vital to their diets, which may, in turn, have led to the Clovis's disappearance from the North American continent.

The main food of the Folsom, whom scientists believe followed the Clovis, was the ancient bison, an animal that was more massive than

Thomas Moran painted In the Teton Range *in 1899.*

WYOMING'S MEDICINE WHEEL

On the top of Medicine Mountain, east of Lovell, is a mysterious rock formation left over from prehistoric times. It is believed to be the remnant of some kind of medicine wheel that may have been used in an ancient ceremony. The formation consists of rocks laid out to look like 28 spokes of a wheel that has a 245-foot circumference.

the modern-day bison. The Folsom chiseled spearheads that have been found throughout Wyoming. These weapons are thinner and smaller than those used by the Clovis, probably due to the smaller size of the animals that the Folsom people hunted.

By the time the Plano arrived the main focus of the hunt was the ancestor of the modern-day bison, a smaller animal than those hunted by the Clovis and Folsom. There is evidence that some of the Plano people were semisedentary, settling down for certain periods of the year rather than constantly migrating. Scientists have also found evidence that the Plano people hunted in groups, which, in turn, suggests that they had a stronger sense of community than earlier groups of people did.

HISTORIC NATIVE AMERICANS

The next groups of people who arrived in what is now Wyoming were the ancestors of modern-day Native Americans. They included people from various tribes, such as the Arapaho, Arikara, Bannock, Blackfeet, Cheyenne, Crow, Gros Ventre, Kiowa, Nez Perce, Sheep Eater, Sioux, Shoshone, and Ute. These people, for the most part, were nomadic, traveling across the plains in search of food. Many of these people followed the trails of the extensive herds of bison, using bison meat to nourish their bodies and bison hides to clothe themselves and to make their portable living shelters, or tepees. It was these early tribes of people who invented the bow and arrow to improve their hunting. Slowly, many of these groups joined together to become larger tribes, sharing their common cultures. Of all the tribes who either lived or passed through the area that now comprises Wyoming, the Arapaho, Shoshone, and the Cheyenne were the most prominent.

Early Native Americans in Wyoming were nomadic, setting up temporary shelters as they crossed the plains.

HUNTING BISON

Early Native Americans did not have horses, so they had to hunt on foot. Some tribal people used dogs to assist them in the hunt, as they herded large numbers of bison toward a steep cliff. Once the bison were running, it was all but impossible for them to stop, and many would fall over the edge. The introduction of horses by the Spanish, sometime around 1730, made hunting bison much easier. The native people rode on their ponies alongside the bison and used spears and bows and arrows to make their kill.

Before the Arapaho moved to the northeastern corner of what would become Wyoming, they were not nomadic. They worked the land as farmers. The Arapaho were known as a rather peaceful tribe, and they were more willing than some other tribes to accommodate the settlers who began to appear on their land.

The Wyoming Shoshone migrated from the area that would become the state of Utah and settled along the eastern slopes of the Rockies in what was referred to as Warm Valley (which later became the Wind River Reservation, where their descendents now live). Unlike the Arapaho, the Shoshone had always been a nomadic tribe, following herds of bison, deer, and elk.

The Cheyenne may have migrated from the Great Lakes area, where they had lived in established communities. Once they migrated south and west, however, they, too, became nomadic. They eventually created an alliance with the Arapaho to have a greater force against enemy tribes. Because these early Native Americans passed along their history through oral renditions, rather than writing about their past, details about these older cultures are found only through archaeological discoveries and by visiting modern-day descendants of these people and listening to their tribal stories.

OUTSIDERS ARRIVE

Nobody knows for sure when the first European people entered Wyoming. Some historians suggest that the first to reach Wyoming might have been French-Canadian explorer François Louis Verendrye. However, we do know that between 1804 and 1806 John Colter, who was part of the Lewis and Clark expedition, left the group as it returned east so he could scout the Yellowstone and Teton areas. Although other explorers may have come before him, Colter was the first person who told about his experiences in what would become the Wyoming area.

Colter's stories were exciting and aroused the interest of more explorers, who packed up their gear and headed to what would one day become Wyoming. Fur trappers soon followed. Next came fur traders, who exchanged supplies and money with the Native Americans for pelts. For the most part, Native Americans had good relations with the first arrivals. They exchanged the fur pelts they collected for guns, compasses, and other tools that they needed. Some Native Americans also intermarried with the settlers, thus making the best of the situation as one culture learned from the other.

Following in the fur traders' steps, a growing number of settlers began to make the cross-country journey. Most planned to settle in Oregon and California, so they needed to find a route that would safely carry them across the Rockies. The fur traders had explored possible routes to the West Coast and knew that there were very few places where a wagon could cross the mountains. However, one of the best places turned out to be located in present-day Wyoming. The best gap in the long wall of mountains was at South Pass in southwest Wyoming. That is how the Oregon Trail, the most important path to the West Coast, came to cross Wyoming. Travelers entered the future state at Fort Laramie, the last place

Elizabeth Lochrie depicts fur trappers and Native Americans trading pelts for supplies in The Fur Trappers.

Emigrants on the Oregon Trail passed through Wyoming on their journey west.

to buy supplies before crossing the mountains. Weeks later, as the once-distant peaks grew closer, the settlers would camp in the shadows of a great rock rising from the plains called Independence Rock. Many travelers carved their names and the date they stopped into the granite there. This early graffiti assured the friends and family members who followed them that they had made it safely to that point and had continued west.

CROSSING THE CONTINENTAL DIVIDE

South Pass, Wyoming, was one of the most important landmarks on the Oregon Trail. South Pass is a 20-mile-wide valley (or "saddle") that passes through the Continental Divide, located in southwest Wyoming about 35 miles south/southwest of Lander. The Lewis and Clark expedition did not know about this relatively easy way to cross the Rockies, since the pass was not discovered until 1812, when Robert Stuart, of the Pacific Fur Company, returned through South Pass on his way back east from Astoria, Oregon. Stuart and his small band of men had heard of warring Native Americans who made any other familiar crossing dangerous. They came upon South Pass by accident when they turned south to find another way to get across the mountains. Stuart published his findings only in France, so the new route remained a secret to other settlers. Then, in 1824, explorer and fur trapper Jedediah Smith came across it. This time the news spread, and eight years later, Benjamin Bonneville took the first caravan of wagons over the pass. Today visitors can take Wyoming State Highway 28 across the pass and see the remaining wagon ruts that run alongside the highway (above).

Each year the traffic increased. Mormons began using the trail to reach the religious community they were building at Salt Lake City, Utah. Gold was discovered in California in 1848, and traffic on the trail mushroomed. Before the flow stopped, a quarter of a million travelers had made the journey.

SACAGAWEA

Sacagawea, a Shoshone woman from what would later become Wyoming, was crucial to the Lewis and Clark expedition during its journey across the West.

Sacagawea was born around 1784. When she was a child, she was captured by the Hidatsa and taken away from her own people. She married a French explorer and lived in the Dakotas until 1805, when Lewis and Clark arrived and asked her to guide their expedition.

Sacagawea ably brought the expedition through country she had not seen since childhood and helped negotiate safe passage for the Lewis and Clark group with the Shoshone. She led Lewis and Clark all the way to the Pacific Ocean and then back through the Yellowstone area as they returned east. Lewis and Clark later described Sacagawea's courageous help, making her a historic figure.

Little is known of the rest of Sacagawea's life. Some stories say she reappeared as an elderly woman on Wyoming's Wind River Reservation, where she died in 1884.

WAR BETWEEN NATIVE AMERICANS AND SETTLERS

Few of the early travelers on the Oregon Trail stayed in what would become Wyoming (unless you count the bodies of those who died during the brutal journey). Nevertheless, the increasingly heavy traffic on the trail upset the way of life of the Native Americans who lived there. The noise and presence of the travelers, the hunting for food or sport, and the destruction of plants drove away the wildlife on which the Native Americans depended to exist. And then newcomers—particularly traders, gold prospectors, and the soldiers sent to protect them—began to settle in present-day Wyoming, taking possession of the land that the native population had long used as hunting grounds.

In the 1860s tension between whites and Native Americans boiled over in the country surrounding the Oregon Trail, which ran through the heart of the Native-American hunting grounds. Army massacres of Native Americans in what would later become northern Colorado and southern Idaho killed hundreds of people. Native Americans struck back in a series of attacks on soldiers and settlers, which sometimes completely stopped wagon traffic on the Oregon Trail. Distraught over the recurring massacres by U.S. forces as well as a dwindling supply of food due to the loss of their hunting grounds and broken promises by the U.S. government, in 1866 a group of Lakota, together with some Arapaho and Cheyenne, were led by Chief Red Cloud, who surprised a regiment of the U.S. cavalry near Fort Phil Kearny in present-day northern Wyoming and killed all eighty-one of them in a bloody fight. The Native-American victory inspired other tribes to try in earnest to rid their land of white people.

After two more years of smaller battles, a treaty signed in 1868 at Fort Laramie gave the Native Americans promises of freedom. The Native Americans agreed to allow roads and railroads to be built, and the U.S. government promised to set aside a large reservation for Native Americans in what is now western South Dakota and to keep new settlers from going there.

RED CLOUD—WYOMING NATIVE-AMERICAN LEADER

Red Cloud (1822–1909) is remembered as both a warrior and a statesman and as one of the most important Native-American leaders of the late nineteenth century. Between 1866 and 1868 Red Cloud launched one of the most successful rebellions against the U.S. government, becoming the first (and the last) Native-American leader to defeat the U.S. cavalry. Although other tribes continued to wage war against those who were invading their land, after 1868 Red Cloud used more diplomatic measures. He fought for the rights of all Native Americans, bringing pressure upon corrupt government officials who broke their promises, sold the natives tainted food, and otherwise deprived Native Americans of their rights.

WASHAKIE—A GREAT DIPLOMAT

Many Native-American leaders played important roles during the decades of contact and conflict with newcomers from the east. One was the great Shoshone chief Washakie, whose valor has been the subject of many stories. Legend has it that after years of fighting between the Shoshone and Crow over who could hunt on the lands surrounding Crowheart Butte, Washakie challenged the Crow chief to settle the matter once and for all. Washakie won the battle. But Washakie is mainly remembered not as a warrior but as a diplomat—a peacemaker between the Shoshone and the settlers. Washakie knew that the settlers would not go away. Instead of mourning the loss of the Shoshone's nomadic way of life, Washakie worked to secure land and to return his people to the agricultural lifestyle they had known centuries earlier.

At age eighty, Chief Washakie told Wyoming territorial governor John Hoyt of his anguish over the American government's treatment of the Shoshone:

The white man, who possesses this whole vast country from sea to sea, who roams over it at pleasure, and lives where he likes, cannot know the cramp we feel in this little spot, with the underlying remembrance of the fact . . . that every foot of what you proudly call America, not very long ago belonged to the red man.

The white man's government promised that if we, the Shoshones, would be content with the little patch allowed us, it would keep us well supplied with everything necessary to comfortable living, and would see that no white man should cross our borders for our game, or anything else that is ours. But it has not kept its word! The white man kills our game, captures our furs, and sometimes feeds his herds upon our meadows. . . . Knowing all this, do you wonder, sir, that we have fits of depression and think to be avenged!

Washakie worked hard to keep the Shoshone out of the bloody conflicts of the 1850s and 1860s. He negotiated the treaty that created the Wind River Indian Reservation and built trust between his tribe and the U.S. government. When war again broke out between the U.S. army and the Lakota in the mid-1870s, Washakie led more than two hundred Shoshone warriors into battle against the Lakotas. He was in his seventies, yet he continued to assist the army as a scout for twenty more years. Washakie died in 1900. He had compromised more than other Indian leaders, but the Shoshone probably suffered less as a result of his actions. Washakie died a disappointed man, however, because his people would never again enjoy the freedom that they had had before the arrival of the settlers.

A RAILROAD CREATES A TERRITORY

In the half-century before the Fort Laramie Treaty of 1868 the newcomers from the east had transformed life in what would later become Wyoming. But the events of the next few years made all those changes seem small. The reason was the coming of the railroad. The U.S. government wanted trains to replace wagon travel on slow, hazardous roads like the Oregon Trail. The rail route had to be fairly flat, and it had to be close to supplies of coal and water that were needed to fuel the steam locomotives that pulled the trains. The Union Pacific Railroad chose a route across southern Wyoming that had all of these advantages.

Fur trappers had brought trading posts to the area of Wyoming, and the Oregon Trail had brought military forts. However, it was the railroad that brought the cities. Cheyenne, Laramie, Rawlins, Rock Springs, Green River, and Evanston all grew up practically overnight along the rails. At first these places looked more like campgrounds than permanent towns—most of the first so-called buildings were actually tents.

Cities and towns developed across Wyoming as a result of the railroad.

RACIAL TEMPERS FLARE

The Union Pacific Railroad employed many people who were living in what would become the state of Wyoming in the coal mines that the railroad operated to fuel its trains. The miners' lives were difficult, and the pay was poor. In 1875 the miners went on strike, demanding better working conditions. The Union Pacific fired the strikers and replaced them with workers imported from China.

Chinese laborers, who were unaware of how much money they could have made, were willing to work for the railroad's low wages, and they did not join the miners' labor unions. Chinese workers, therefore, helped the railroad owners make big profits. However, the willingness of the Chinese to bend to the demands of the owners made the striking laborers angry. So they blamed the Chinese for their failed strike and their pitiful wages. This, naturally, created tension between the races, and tempers flared quite easily. Then one day in 1885 near Rock Springs, a fight broke out between the whites and the Chinese. This disruption quickly turned into a riot. Fueled by racial prejudice the crowd of whites killed twenty-eight Chinese workers and injured fifteen others. Hundreds of Chinese were driven out of town, and their homes were set on fire.

Sixteen men were arrested for participating in the Rock Springs massacre, but none was ever brought to trial because a grand jury refused to charge them. Governor Francis E. Warren called the massacre "the most damnable and brutal outrage that ever occurred in any country," but few other local whites sympathized with the Chinese. After the massacre, most of the Chinese left the territory.

People streamed in from the east to fill the cities, some coming to work on the railroad, others to open businesses and to buy the best land. Still, others were prospectors searching for gold. They found a little gold near South Pass, which lured a new wave of fortune-seekers into the area. They also discovered a lot of coal, which was mined to fuel the trains. And thus the population of the territory continued to climb. By the time the railroad through what would become Wyoming was complete, there would be approximately 11,000 people living in the area. Ten years later that number would double.

In the same year that the railroad was completed, in 1868, Wyoming belonged to the Dakota Territory. Officials complained to the U.S. government that it was too difficult to rule Wyoming from the Dakotas, so they petitioned for Wyoming to become a separate territory, which it did. When Wyoming's first legislature met in 1869 one of the first laws it passed gave women the right to vote. Nowhere else in the world did women have this liberty. Women's rights leader Susan B. Anthony declared, "Wyoming is the first place on God's green earth which could consistently claim to be the land of the free."

One reason Wyoming gave women the right to vote was because it was eager to attract more people from the east—especially women. In 1870 six out of seven settlers were men, and many of them were lonely. However, few new settlers came to Wyoming until gold was discovered in the Black Hills near the Dakota-Wyoming border. By 1875 thousands of prospectors were invading the Native-American territory that had been established by the Fort Laramie Treaty just seven years earlier.

The U.S. government could do little to keep prospectors away from this protected land, and a new war broke out. In November 1876 Colonel R. S. MacKenzie destroyed a Cheyenne encampment along

THE EQUALITY STATE

Wyoming is called the Equality State because it was the first place to grant women the right to vote. Wyoming women have achieved a remarkable number of other political "firsts":

Esther Morris was appointed the world's first female justice of the peace in 1870 in South Pass City.

Eliza Stewart became the first woman ever to serve on a jury in 1870. This was such a big event that King Wilhelm I of Prussia sent a telegram to President Ulysses S. Grant congratulating him.

Estelle Reel was elected Wyoming's superintendent of education in 1894, making her the first woman to win a statewide election in the United States.

Susan Wissler became Wyoming's first female mayor in 1911, even though she declared she didn't want the job. The townspeople of Dayton ignored that and elected her anyway! She was reelected twice.

In 1920 the town of Jackson elected the country's first all-woman government.

In 1925 Nellie Tayloe Ross became the first female governor in the United States.

the Powder River. Deprived of food and shelter many Native Americans froze or starved to death. The survivors fled to Montana or surrendered and agreed to live on much smaller reservations. This marked the end of Native-American control of the plains.

HOME ON THE RANGE

With most Native Americans forced from their lands, the Wyoming territory entered a new era. The vast rangelands were perfect for raising cattle, and the Union Pacific Railroad was perfect for transporting the cattle to markets in the cities back east. The age of the cowboy had begun.

In just a few years cattle ranches sprouted up all over the Wyoming Territory's eastern plains. The area's population increased as more easterners arrived, eager to own ranches or to work as cowboys.

Soon the rangeland was actually crowded. In some places the grass could not grow back as rapidly as the cattle chewed it. During the hard winter of 1886–1887 disaster struck. The weather was so cold and the snow so deep that the cattle could not find water and food. Hundreds of thousands of cows died. The cattle business did not go bust, but its boom years were over.

Wyoming's vast territory was perfect for raising cattle, attracting those with the cowboy spirit.

LAW AND DISORDER

Twenty years after Wyoming became a territory its population had climbed to over 60,000. Many clamored for the U.S. Congress to grant Wyoming full statehood. They got their wish on July 10, 1890, when Wyoming became the nation's forty-fourth state.

The new state was now responsible for its own law and order, but this was not easy. For years rustlers had been stealing cattle from the open rangelands. Now the cattle barons who owned the largest ranches accused smaller ranchers of this crime. In 1892 a group of gunmen, hired by the big ranchers, killed two people whom the large cattle owners suspected of rustling in Johnson County. Their neighbors armed themselves and surrounded the group, who had holed up at a nearby ranch. The neighbors were preparing to blow up the ranch when U.S. soldiers arrived to rescue the group. Wyomingites, like journalist Asa Mercer, were outraged. "The invasion," Mercer wrote, "was the crowning infamy of the ages."

Ranching continued to grow as Wyomingites discovered that their state's rangelands were just as good for raising sheep as cattle. Sheep ranches began competing for space on the plains. Cattle ranchers pressured the sheepherders to stay out of areas they used to graze cattle. Sheep ranchers pointed out that the open range was owned by the government and that everyone had an equal right to use it. For years, the cattle barons' masked gunmen had a new target. They harassed the sheep ranches, shooting or dynamiting herds of sheep—and sometimes killing sheepherders, too. Finally, seven cattlemen were arrested in 1909 for killing sheep ranchers near the town of Ten Sleep. Five of them went to jail, and the violence mostly ended. Even today, though, there remains tension between cattlemen and sheep ranchers.

GOOD-BYE, OLD PAINT

The cowboy—the sentimental cowboy—sang this sad farewell song at the end of a rare evening in town. It was the last waltz, and as he saddled up Old Paint (his horse) and headed back to the lonesome ranch, he never knew if there would be a next time.

Good - bye, old paint, I'm a - leav - ing Chey - enne. Good -

bye, old paint, I'm a - leav - ing Chey - enne.

Fine

Verse

I'm a - leav - ing Chey - enne,_____ I'm bound for Mon -

tan'. Good-bye, old paint, I'm a-leav-ing Chey-enne._____

D. C. al Fine

POPULATION GROWTH: 1870–2000

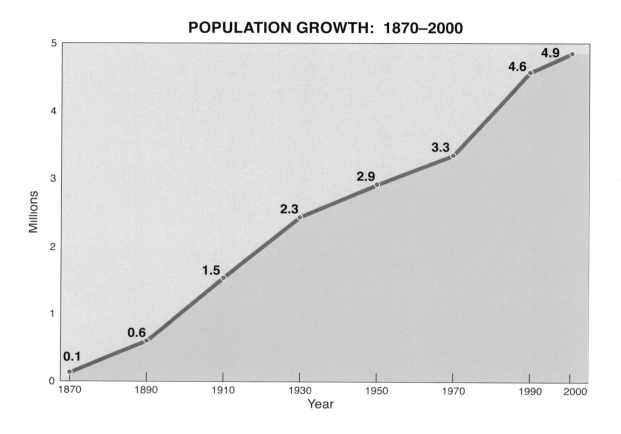

INTO THE TWENTIETH AND TWENTY-FIRST CENTURY

By 1900 Wyoming's population was over 90,000, and twenty years later that figure had doubled. Coal mining and oil drilling were booming, and that brought people and money to the state. In 1914 the state was producing six million barrels of crude oil every year for America's growing fleet of automobiles. That amount increased twofold during World War I, as Wyoming supplied fuel for the nation's war effort.

But wartime prosperity did not last long. The Great Depression, which rocked America during the 1930s, began even earlier in Wyoming.

During the early 1900s those seeking work poured into Wyoming in hope of securing a job in the mining industry.

The state's livestock, coal, and oil industries all suffered from falling prices during the 1920s. Farmers and ranchers endured droughts, coal producers were shut down by strikes, and the oil industry faced stiff competition from other states. Since these industries made up most of Wyoming's economy the whole state was troubled. More than half the state's banks closed during the 1920s, costing some Wyomingites all their savings—a calamity that the rest of the country would face a decade later.

The one bright spot was the rise in tourism. Americans in more prosperous states had discovered the natural beauty of Wyoming, and by the 1920s, automobiles could take them there. This was the time of the flourishing of dude ranches, which gave tourists a taste of the cowboy's life.

With the invention of the automobile, tourists were able to visit Wyoming's natural wonders.

When the nationwide depression hit in the early 1930s Wyoming's hard times got worse. By 1933, 20,000 Wyomingites were unemployed, and Wyoming relied more than almost any other state on government assistance. Even cattle ranchers, whose land and livestock were once worth millions of dollars, received federal money to keep them from going out of business.

When the United States entered World War II in 1941 Wyoming again contributed raw materials to the war effort, particularly oil, coal, and beef. Near Douglas, a prisoner-of-war camp was built, which was soon filled with Italian and German prisoners.

When World War II ended in 1945 prosperity returned to Wyoming and the rest of the country. The war had defeated the Great Depression, and the state's beef and minerals brought good prices again. Coal and oil replaced cattle as Wyoming's most important products. Wyoming's large deposits of uranium, used to run nuclear power plants and to make nuclear weapons, also contributed to the state's postwar boom.

But in the 1980s oil, coal, and uranium prices tumbled, and many young workers moved out of the state in search of jobs. "Rather than choose Wyoming's way," says Paul Krza, a Wyomingite who moved to Colorado, "many residents, especially the young, choose the highway."

Today, energy prices are up, and Wyoming's economy is doing better. In recent years the number of new jobs has increased steadily, and with the new push by the U.S. government to become independent of foreign oil supplies, Wyoming's natural energy resources are becoming more and more attractive and profitable. Wyoming jobs in mining and natural resources enjoyed one of the biggest surges in employment in 2006 along with work in the construction industry.

Today, Wyoming's mining and natural resource industry is thriving.

With almost three million visitors coming annually to Wyoming to enjoy the natural beauty of Yellowstone and the Grand Teton national parks, the economic outlook is good. The word is also getting out that Wyoming is a great place to live. It was ranked, in 2006, as the sixth most livable state in the Union. Wyoming has one of the lowest rankings in crime (forty-seventh) and one of the higher rankings in per capita personal income (twelfth).

Like every state Wyoming also has it challenges. Legislators are wrangling over issues involving the conflicts between wildlife conservation and state ranchers, environmental issues and the effects of mining, drug use, and the need to provide the state's young population with a good education and jobs. One thing that most people would agree with, however, is that Wyoming is a beautiful place to live. And few would argue that the best thing is for everyone to do what they can to keep it that way.

Chapter Three

Life in the Cowboy State

Living in Wyoming is different from living in any other state. "It's not dull, not humdrum, not 'average,'" Wyoming author Nathaniel Burt once claimed. There are so few people, and so much room. Many Wyomingites balance these two facts in remarkable ways. They celebrate the land by working and playing close to it, and they cherish one another and strive to keep far-flung communities together and long-time friendships intact.

CITIES AND TOWNS

Contrary to what many outsiders think, the typical Wyomingite doesn't live in a rustic cabin in the wilderness. For most people living in this state home is in a city or town. Life in Wyoming's larger cities is a lot like city life in other parts of the country. Neighborhoods in Casper and Cheyenne would not look out of place in most other cities of the same size. Kids attend schools and hang out at shopping malls like children in any other state.

Smaller towns are more likely to fit the image of rugged, historic Wyoming. Towns like Buffalo, home to 3,900 people on the northeastern

Wyomingites' work and play often come together, as can be seen by this rodeo clown.

plains, have preserved the flavor of life from half a century ago or more. Buffalo's Main Street is lined with old brick buildings. Faded signs still adorn their sides, showing that they were once hotels and banks. Now, however, they are more likely to be art galleries, antique shops, and restaurants.

Some Wyoming towns are little more than a mishmash of gas stations, fast-food restaurants, and mobile homes spreading from the old town center. Even those who really love these towns admit that they are not beautiful. But they are often busy places, home to many unmarried workers as well as young families.

Regardless of their individual characters, Wyoming towns are outposts on the open land. For rural Wyomingites going to town may mean visiting a community of only several hun- dred people, a place that happens to have a grocery store, a video store, a church, a bar, or a restau- rant where people can gather. For teens, a town might also be a place to skateboard—most farms and ranches do not have long stretches of pavement.

Wyomingites cherish the elbow room that their remote towns and ranches provide them. This is why the automobile is such an impor- tant part of life in Wyoming. Forget about horses—Wyoming has the highest rate of motor vehicle ownership in the country.

Towns in Wyoming tend to be small and located near rural, open land.

POPULATION DENSITY

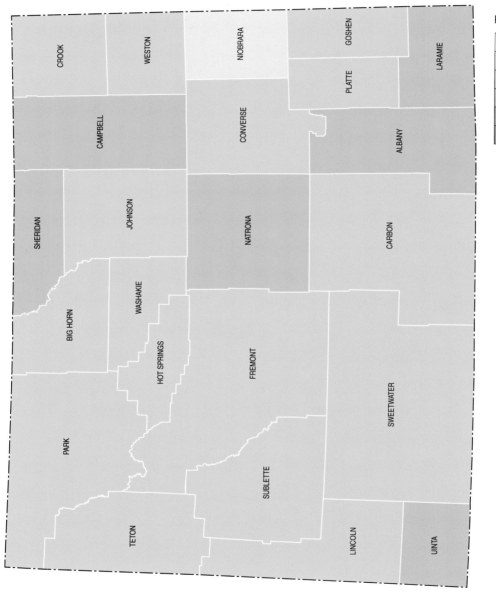

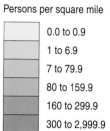

Persons per square mile

- 0.0 to 0.9
- 1 to 6.9
- 7 to 79.9
- 80 to 159.9
- 160 to 299.9
- 300 to 2,999.9

CROOK

WESTON

NIOBRARA

GOSHEN

LARAMIE

PLATTE

CAMPBELL

CONVERSE

ALBANY

SHERIDAN

JOHNSON

NATRONA

CARBON

BIG HORN

WASHAKIE

HOT SPRINGS

FREMONT

SWEETWATER

PARK

SUBLETTE

TETON

LINCOLN

UINTA

THROUGH THE SEASONS

Many Wyoming towns plan festivals and events for the winter months. The International Rocky Mountain Stage Stop Sled Dog Race takes place over more than a week on a 400-mile course that visits towns in Wyoming's southwestern corner. The towns are resting points at the end of each race day, and the arrival of the exhausted sledders and their dogs sparks a celebration each night. In tiny Alpine, three hundred tickets have been sold for the banquet to welcome the racers (several times more than the population of the entire town). While the sled drivers eat with the townspeople, the dogs wolf down concoctions of beef, chicken, fish, and vitamins to restore their strength for the next day's racing.

Some Wyomingites take advantage of the frigid temperatures by participating in the International Rocky Mountain Stage Stop Sled Dog Race.

KIDS AND CARS

Wyoming is a state of great distances. Some children ride the bus 75 miles each way to school. They can finish all their homework on the bus before they get home!

Wyoming allows fourteen-year-olds to get driver's licenses if they need them to get to school. On private land, children are permitted to drive at any age and often do.

Even with such lively events Wyoming winters can be long and lonely. Hundreds of miles of roads are routinely closed all winter because of snow. Many more miles of roads get shut down temporarily when snowstorms and wind make them impassable—even Wyoming's three interstate highways, its major ties to the outside world, are often closed off.

But winter weather is more an adventure than a disaster for Wyomingites. It makes the state one of the nation's finest spots for skiing and snowmobiling. Serious skiers consider the Jackson Hole Ski Resort to be among the best in the world, and even beginners, gazing across the valley at the Teton Range, can tell that it is one of the most beautiful. Snowmobiling is even more popular than skiing. Wyoming has a large network of snowmobile trails, many reaching wild areas that are far from the nearest roads. A common roadside scene in the winter is rows of four-wheel-drive trucks parked at trailheads. The empty snowmobile trailers behind them show how many groups are out gunning through the thick snowdrifts. Some accuse these snowmobile riders of disturbing wildlife, which has a hard enough time searching for food in the deep snow. "That's nonsense," one sledder claims. "Our sleds are like snowplows.

A daring skier flies off a cliff in Jackson Hole.

Animals use the trails we make to move around and find food." Other people believe that the noise and pollution from the snowmobiles are bad for the people who come to see the quiet, snow-frosted landscape as well as the wild animals. Debate over this issue continues in the U.S. Congress, which has, in the past, curtailed or banned snowmobiles outright from national parks.

Springtime in Wyoming gradually brings longer and warmer days. The snow begins to melt all across the state. Spring is calving season, and ranch families work many hours to make sure the newborn lambs and calves are safe. As the grass thickens and warm spring breezes blow, wild animals fatten themselves after the hard winter months.

Summer is short in Wyoming, so people make the most of it. Farmers plant their crops as early as possible and hope for rain. School ends, but many kids settle down to hard work rather than relaxation and television, because Wyoming families tend to work together to get by. Summer is also the busiest time for visiting and celebrating. It is a time of county fairs and the Wyoming State Fair in Douglas.

Wyoming's biggest celebration is Frontier Days, held every July in Cheyenne. Thousands of people attend pancake breakfasts and chili feasts, enjoy the carnival rides, and watch air shows. There is a Native-American village run by the Shoshone tribe, with displays of traditional dancing and storytelling, and booths offering crafts and food. But the festival's high point is its rodeo, the oldest one in the United States. A rodeo's main events are bronco and steer riding, in which contestants try to stay atop the wild, bucking animals for as long as possible. There are also contests to see how quickly competitors can rope and tie calves and steers. Rodeos also sport races to see how fast a horse and rider can run figure-eights around closely spaced barrels. All these events test traditional cowboy skills (and cowgirl skills, too—many competitors are women).

A Wyoming cowboy competes at the Frontier Days Rodeo in Cheyenne.

Summer never seems to last long enough in Wyoming. Children return reluctantly to school; farmers spend long days harvesting their crops. Fall is hunting season, though, and Wyoming is full of wildlife. Thousands of people come from other states to hunt antelope, deer, elk, and moose. Strangely, hunting is not particularly popular among Wyomingites. Only about one in ten is a hunter, a much lower rate than in many other places. Fishing, on the other hand, is very popular. In Riverton and Casper four in ten residents consider themselves frequent anglers.

As winter rolls around again Wyomingites—whose whole way of life revolves around the outdoorst—end to retreat indoors once again.

Even in the winter, though, Wyomingites are active, sometimes in ways that don't fit their frontier image. Wyoming ranks second among the states in the percentage of people who run or jog, and third in the proportion of bicyclists. Wyomingites also visit health clubs and gymnasiums far more frequently than the average American. Along with the tough, active work that most residents do, this makes Wyoming one of the most physically fit states in the nation.

High school sports are also important, especially in Wyoming's smaller communities. In Gillette the girls' volleyball, cross-country, and swimming teams are often nationally ranked. The girls' basketball team is so good that it travels around the country playing in national tournaments.

When warm weather nears, many Wyomingites head to the rivers and streams to fish.

COWBOY BISCUITS AND ICE CREAM

Hard work builds powerful appetites, so Wyomingites enjoy hearty meals. Here's a Wyoming dessert that is best eaten in a ranch kitchen during a howling blizzard, but you can enjoy it anywhere. Ask an adult to help you with this recipe.

2 cups flour
4 teaspoons baking powder
1 teaspoon salt
2 tablespoons butter
3/4 cup milk
1 can sliced peaches in syrup
1 carton vanilla ice cream

Preheat the oven to 450 degrees Fahrenheit. Mix the dry ingredients in a bowl and sift them. Work the butter into the mixture with your fingertips. Add the milk gradually, stirring with a knife to make a soft dough. (If it seems too stiff, add a little more milk.)

On a floured board, flatten the dough to half an inch thick. Use a drinking glass to cut out biscuits (dip the glass in flour between cuts so it doesn't stick). Place the biscuits on a buttered cookie sheet and bake until golden brown (12 to 15 minutes).

As soon as the biscuits are done, it's time for dessert. Open a can of sliced peaches in syrup. Place a hot biscuit in a bowl. Surround it with two or three peach slices. Top this with a scoop or two of vanilla ice cream, and drizzle it with a spoonful of the syrup from the peaches. Enjoy it while it's still hot—and cold!

THE FACE OF THE HISTORIC WILD WEST

William F. Cody, or "Buffalo Bill," earned his nickname from a dark part of his career—his role in the slaughter of the bison herds. But he was also a scout and an entertainer, and his Wild West Show made him the West's best-known figure by the end of the nineteenth century.

Buffalo Bill's father died when Bill was eleven, and Bill got a job as a messenger to help support his family. Later he became a rider for the Pony Express, a mail delivery service, and he once galloped on his horse for 320 miles in less than one day—the longest Pony Express ride ever. During the Civil War Buffalo Bill was a Union army scout. Afterward he became a hunter, supplying meat to the crews building the transcontinental railroad. This is when he became famous as "Buffalo Bill," the greatest bison hunter in the West.

Buffalo Bill is honored at Wyoming's Buffalo Bill Historical Center.

His exploits during the Indian wars of the 1860s caught the attention of eastern newspapers, and Buffalo Bill became a national celebrity. He put together his Wild West Show, which toured the United States and Europe, dazzling audiences with its romantic displays of life on the frontier. Annie Oakley, a crack pistol shooter, and even the defeated Lakota chief Sitting Bull joined the show. Buffalo Bill and Sitting Bull, enemies in war, became friends in peace.

Buffalo Bill's show made him rich. He bought a ranch east of Yellowstone Park and helped establish the nearby town of Cody—named, of course, after him. But the hunter, scout, and showman was no businessman. The Wild West Show went bankrupt, and Buffalo Bill died almost broke. According to the Buffalo Bill Museum in Colorado, Bill requested to be buried on top of Lookout Mountain, about a thirty-minute drive outside of Denver, in 1917. Lookout Mountain is now a part of the Denver Mountain Parks System.

OUTLAWS

Two of Wyoming's most famous characters were its most notorious outlaws, Butch Cassidy and the Sundance Kid. Cassidy started his life of crime as a cattle rustler (or thief) but soon found bank and train robbery more profitable. He joined Harry Longabaugh (the Sundance Kid) and other desperadoes to form the Hole-in-the-Wall Gang, named after a favorite hideout near Kaycee.

Cassidy was caught stealing horses near Lander in 1894 and spent two years in prison. When he was released his gang went back to its old ways. By 1901 the law was closing in on Cassidy again, so he and the Sundance Kid fled to South America, where they continued robbing banks and trains. Some say the pair perished in a shoot-out in Bolivia, but others claim they returned to live out their lives in Wyoming. Francis Smith, a Wyoming doctor, remembered how an old man appeared in his doorway in the 1920s. "You don't know who I am, do you?" asked the man. "You look familiar," replied the doctor, "but I can't quite say." The man displayed a surgical scar on his belly, which the doctor recognized as his own work. His face had been altered by plastic surgery, but, Smith insisted, the man was Butch Cassidy.

NATIVE AMERICANS: THE OLDEST WYOMINGITES

Early Native Americans (and their ancestors) lived in Wyoming before it was Wyoming. The Great Plains offered excellent hunting and room to roam, which they did as they followed the wildlife, as well as the seasons, moving from place to place and setting up temporary camps along the way. They lived fairly good but rugged lives, taking what bounty they needed to survive and then leaving the land and its creatures to rebound, almost as if the native people had never been there. Their lifestyle changed dramatically, however, when trappers and settlers began moving into their territory. Life became more and more stressful as wars were fought over the right to the land and all that went with it. Native Americans were brave and fought hard, but they did not have the numbers or the weaponry the whites had and eventually they were either pushed out of the state or forced to live on reservations. The Shoshone were placed on the reservation at Wind River in 1863. The Arapaho were sent there eight years later.

Today, Wind River is the only reservation in Wyoming. It is located in the center of the state. With its headquarters at Fort Washakie, Wind River Reservation is home to some 2,600 Eastern Shoshone and 5,000 Northern Arapaho. It is the seventh-largest reservation in the United States. These two tribes live together on two million acres.

Some believe that two legendary figures are buried on the reservation: Chief Washakie and Sacagawea. Powwows, or dance and culture celebrations, are held on the reservation throughout the summer. The powwows give the Native Americans a chance to celebrate the ancient dances and costumes of their tribes as well as a chance to visit with old friends who come to the reservation during these celebrations. The tribes have built a casino on the reservation,

A Shoshone celebrates his heritage and customs at the Wind River Reservation.

which the public is welcome to visit and enjoy. The reservation makes money from the casino as well as from royalties from the gas and oil produced on their land. Some Native-American families also make a living ranching. The Eastern Shoshone and the Northern Arapaho are the only two federally recognized Native-American tribes in Wyoming. According to the 2000 U.S. Census estimate, there were more than 11,000 Native Americans living in the state.

SETTLERS AND RANCHERS

From the beginning of the nineteenth century white settlers and ranchers have been attracted to the landscape of Wyoming. The land held a lot of promise, which has allowed these mostly European descendants to make a fairly good living. Coming from countries such as Germany, England, Ireland, Sweden, Italy, France, and the Netherlands, the original settlers, many of them first- and second-generation citizens, staked their claims, developed the land, and made themselves a home. The weather was not always friendly and making peace with the original people of the land, the Native Americans, did not always go smoothly, but today the majority of the population of Wyoming is made up of the descendants of these original settlers. The estimated U.S. census figures for 2005 stated that there were more than 450,000 white Wyomingites, making up almost 95 percent of the total population, with over one-fourth of them claiming German ancestry. The next largest group, at about 78,000, were those who claimed English roots. Following that group were 65,000 people who came from Irish stock.

VOLGA-GERMANS EMMIGRATE TO WYOMING

Of the German settlers in Wyoming, most of them were a group called Volga-Germans. This group of Germans actually immigrated to Wyoming from Russia. In the eighteenth century Russian Queen Catherine the Great granted a group of German immigrants the right to settle on the Volga steppes of Russia in exchange for protecting the area from invading Mongolians. The Germans were excellent farmers and eventually turned this part of Russia into a thriving farm community. However, at the turn of the century, many of these Volga-Germans became disheartened by broken promises made by the Russian royalty and decided to look for land and religious freedom somewhere else. Large groups made the journey to the United States, and thousands settled in Wyoming, mostly on the eastern side.

ETHNIC WYOMING

American Indian and Alaska Native
2%

African American
less than 1%

Other
5%

White
93%

Hispanic
7%

Not Hispanic
93%

Note: A person of Cuban, Mexican, Puerto Rican, South or Central American, or other Spanish culture or origin, regardless of race, is defined as Hispanic.

OTHER IMMIGRANTS TO WYOMING

Jobs, natural beauty, and a good living attract newcomers to Wyoming just as they have since Wyoming became a state. Although the percentage of nonwhites living in Wyoming is small, other ethnic groups have been living in Wyoming for a long time.

African Americans

Jobs were a big attraction for the African-American community even back in 1870, about a decade after the Civil War. Opportunities in mining and in the construction of the railroad meant a decent wage. By 1910 there were more than two thousand African Americans living in Wyoming, and they helped create vibrant communities in places such as Casper, Cheyenne, Laramie, Rock Springs, and Sheridan. William Jefferson Hardin, from Laramie County, served in the sixth and seventh legislative assemblies

African Americans make up less than 1 percent of Wyoming's population.

JAPANESE INTERNMENT CAMPS IN WYOMING

During World War II the U.S. government feared that Japanese Americans might collaborate with the Japanese government and work as spies. This fear increased to the point that President Franklin Delano Roosevelt signed a decree that forced thousands of first- and second-generation Japanese Americans to leave their homes, businesses, and most of their possessions behind and to live in internment camps throughout the United States. One of those internment camps was located at Heart Mountain, outside of Cody, Wyoming. During the time of internment (1942–1945), the internment camp housed more than ten thousand Japanese Americans, making it the third-largest Wyoming city at that time. The Japanese Americans lived in rows of dreary, tar-paper barracks surrounded by barbed wire. When they were freed, nearly all of them left Wyoming as quickly as they could. In

1988 Congress paid retribution money to the victims of this misguided wartime policy and issued an apology. Today, the Heart Mountain community is listed on the Registry of Historic Places. Although the Japanese Americans were, for the most part, feared throughout Wyoming, and laws were passed to prohibit a Japanese American from owning land, the Japanese-American internees helped build the Heart Mountain Reclamation Project, which brought water to the arid landscape and in 2007 was providing much-needed water for the crop of barley that grows around the perimeter of the old camp.

from 1879 to 1884, the first African American to do so. Today, there are about four thousand African Americans living in Wyoming.

Hispanics

Hispanics make up the largest and fastest-growing minority group in Wyoming, numbering more than 30,000 and projected to increase in the years to come. Some Hispanics of Mexican descent have lived in Wyoming for a long time. After all, parts of Wyoming belonged to Mexico up until the end of the Mexican War in 1848. It was through the Treaty of Guadalupe that the United States won territorial rights from Mexico over part of Wyoming. Other Mexican Hispanics came to Wyoming from New Mexico and Texas. They were migrant farmers looking for work. As early as 1930 there were more than seven thousand Mexicans living in Wyoming. Mexican laborers and farmers were not always welcome in Wyoming. Segregation was prominent and racial harassment was a way of life for many. Retired teacher and author John Raul Gutiérrez of Gillette, Wyoming, has spent his life as an educator, impressing upon his students the need to reject the stereotypical racial prejudices that others might attempt to inflict on people of color.

Asian Americans

Chinese laborers were brought to Wyoming to work on the railroad in the 1800s. They were also chased out of the state when riots against them broke out in 1885. Then, in the later 1800s, the U.S. government completely disallowed immigrants from Asian countries. After World War II, immigration laws turned in favor of Asian immigration, and the number of Asian Americans has steadily increased in the United States ever since. Although there are nearly 12 million Asian Americans living in the United States, Wyoming's Asian population is less than three thousand, the smallest Asian-American population in the country.

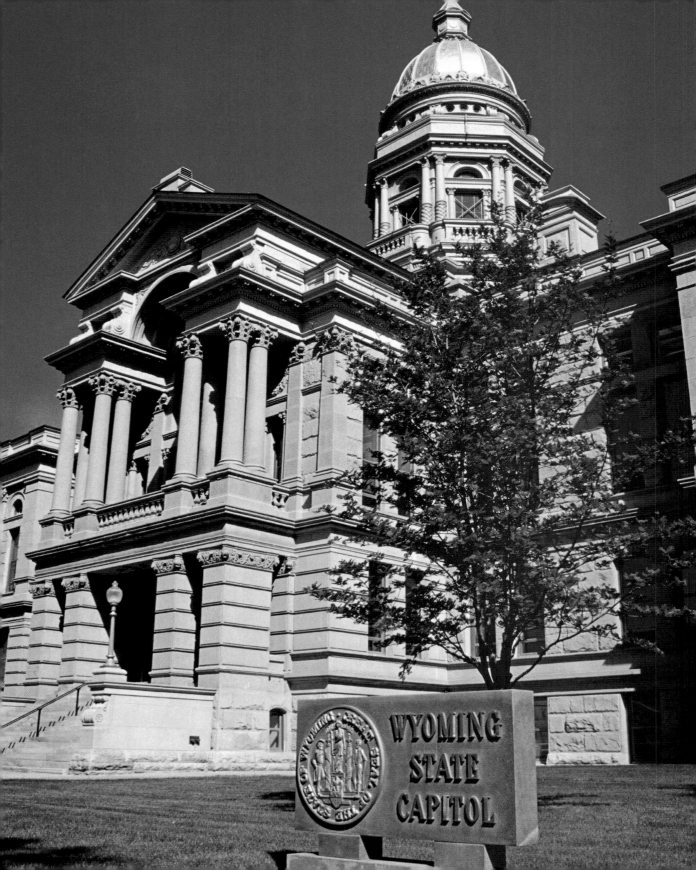

Chapter Four

Governing the Cowboy State

As the Union Pacific Railroad blazed its trail across southern Wyoming in 1868 boomtowns like Cheyenne and Laramie filled with rowdy railroad workers and enough outlaws and desperadoes to make life miserable and dangerous. Citizens often took the law into their own hands, but their vigilante justice was seldom fair. "We're going to give you a fair trial," the villains were promised, "followed by a first-class hanging." It took the establishment of a territorial government in Wyoming to create true law and order, to settle disputes honestly, and to coordinate the projects that have made the state a good place to live today.

INSIDE GOVERNMENT

Wyoming's government is based on the state constitution, which was written in 1889. The constitution can be changed only if two-thirds of the state legislature and a majority of the state's voters approve.

Wyoming's government has three bodies: the executive branch, the legislative branch, and the judicial branch.

Wyoming's constitution calls for three branches of government: executive, legislative, and judicial.

Executive

The executive branch is headed by the governor, who is elected every four years. The governor makes recommendations about which laws the state legislature should pass. Governors can veto laws they do not like, and unless two-thirds of the legislators vote to override a veto, the governor has the final say. Working under the governor are other executive officials, including the secretary of state, the attorney general, and the state treasurer. These officials, and the departments they lead, work out the details of executing the laws—making sure, for example, that Wyoming's schools receive the correct amount of money.

Legislative

The legislative branch consists of a house of representatives and a senate. The house has sixty members who are elected to two-year terms; the thirty senators are elected to four-year terms. All new laws (and changes to old ones) are proposed, discussed, and voted on by these legislators. The legislature meets every January, and its meetings cannot last for more than forty days. This is a shorter session than the legislative sessions of most states, reflecting Wyomingites' wish to restrict government activity.

Judicial

At the top of the judicial branch is a supreme court with five justices. They are appointed by the governor and are subject to a "retention election" in which voters are asked whether the judges should be retained. They serve eight-year terms. The supreme court sometimes clarifies the meaning of vaguely worded laws and decides whether laws violate the state constitution. Wyoming also has nine judicial districts, each with one or two judges, who are appointed by the governor to six-year terms. These courts handle civil and criminal trials and appeals of verdicts reached by county and municipal courts.

Vice President Dick Cheney addressing a joint session of the Wyoming legislature.

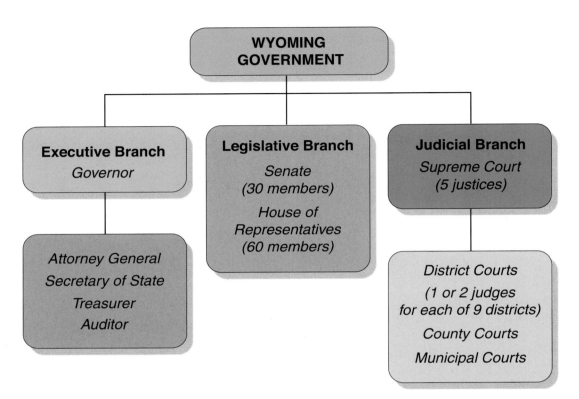

```
                    ┌─────────────────────┐
                    │      WYOMING        │
                    │    GOVERNMENT       │
                    └─────────────────────┘
```

Executive Branch
Governor

Attorney General
Secretary of State
Treasurer
Auditor

Legislative Branch
Senate
(30 members)

House of
Representatives
(60 members)

Judicial Branch
Supreme Court
(5 justices)

District Courts
(1 or 2 judges
for each of 9 districts)
County Courts
Municipal Courts

COWBOY POLITICS

Typically Wyomingites are conservative. They believe that government should be small and its powers should be limited. They think that the federal government is too powerful and wish it had a smaller role in Wyoming. In recent years the majority of Wyoming voters and elected officials have been Republicans.

Today, Wyoming is one of the most Republican states in the country (although it should be noted that Dave Freudenthal is the twelfth Democratic governor to lead the state). Wyomingites prefer to have a lot of freedom in determining how they live. Most oppose laws that make it hard to own a gun, for example. As former senator Alan Simpson put it, "In the Cowboy State, gun control simply means how steady you hold your rifle."

Governor Dave Freudenthal delivers his inaugural speech in Cheyenne on January 2, 2007.

Most Wyomingites agree that taxes should be low. Wyoming is one of the few states that has no income tax, which means it has less money to fund government programs than most other states. A special tax on minerals mined in the state makes up some of the difference. The state has to raise money to pay for everything from building roads and maintaining public schools to managing wildlife and providing assistance to the poor. Still, Wyoming spends more than the national average for police and crime prevention and has one of the lowest crime rates in the country.

Wyoming also spends a lot on education—more money per pupil than any state but Alaska. This is partly because a large proportion of its people are schoolchildren (Wyoming has one of the youngest populations in the country). Another reason is that the population is spread thinly across a lot of space, so the state must run many small schools in remote locations. Willow Creek School, for example, is 25 miles from the nearest town. It has only five students, but the state pays for an aide as well as the teacher. Such schools are obviously more expensive per pupil than big-city schools. However, Willow Creek's students get a lot of attention and score high on math and reading tests—like the rest of Wyoming's kids.

A high level of student achievement is found throughout Wyoming as a result of the department of education's dollars spent per student.

WYOMING BY COUNTY

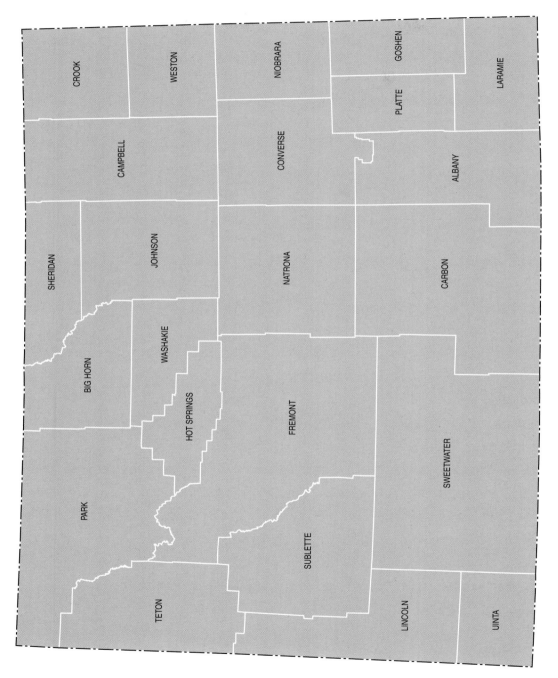

HATHAWAY SCHOLARSHIP PROGRAM

The Hathaway Scholarship Program, named for former Wyoming governor Stanley Hathaway and begun with graduating seniors in 2006, is a great example of Wyoming's legislature working to help students, which, the legislators hope, will also enhance the state's ability to provide a well-educated workforce.

The scholarship program was named for Hathaway because he established a state trust fund through the royalties of Wyoming's mining industry. The principal of the trust fund can never be spent. However, the interest earned on that fund is more than enough to pay for the scholarship program as well as other legislative financial needs. In 2005 the state legislature passed Senate File 122, which established the Hathaway Scholarship. Through this endowment Wyoming high school students who meet certain academic standards may apply for funds to cut the cost of tuition to Wyoming's colleges and university.

In 2006, on average, for every one hundred Wyoming high school freshmen, forty went on to college. Of that forty, however, only nineteen earned a college degree. These figures are just below average for the entire United States. Some senators, in passing the legislature for the Hathaway Scholarship, hoped that the endowment would not only assist students in paying for college but would also create a better-educated population. The reason for this is that the scholarship requires students to maintain a more rigorous curriculum and earn a higher grade point average. The scholarship might inspire students who want to go on to college to become better prepared for the challenge of a higher degree and, thus, the graduation rate might improve. Those who choose not to go to college will also benefit because the high school curriculum will become more intensive and they, too, will be challenged to buckle down and study harder. In a 2007 article from the online publication of the Casper *Star-Tribune*, University of Wyoming professor Andy Hansen stated, "schools nationwide are moving toward more demanding curricula . . . which means Wyoming will need to increase its requirements to keep pace. In today's global marketplace, Wyoming students also will compete against graduates from around the world." So setting the standards higher will be a win-win situation for everyone.

The legislature believes that the Hathaway Scholarship Program will not only inspire Wyoming's students to attend in-state colleges, but will also make it more likely that they will stay in Wyoming after they graduate, using their degrees and applying their knowledge to help keep Wyoming's environment healthy, to solve Wyoming's present and future challenges, to invigorate Wyoming's economy, and possibly to one day run for public office to ensure that Wyoming will maintain a bright and well-informed state and federal legislature.

Chapter Five

Sharing the Riches

Wyoming is fortunate to have rich natural resources. But relying on them for Wyoming's economic well-being is risky. Agricultural and mineral prices rise and fall, and the state's economy rises and falls with them. When prices are high there are plenty of jobs. When prices plummet jobs disappear—and people disappear, too, leaving the state to find jobs.

Today, however, the state's economy is growing, and people are arriving from other states in search of work as Wyoming's legislature, businesses, and universities are working to make the state's economy more varied and Wyomingites' lives more economically successful. Today, most jobs are found in the service industries, which include tourism and professions such as those in the medical field. The second-largest group includes those working in finance, insurance, or real estate. About 20 percent of Wyoming's labor force works for the government, including people who are enlisted in the military. The remaining workforce includes people working in retail (such as at department stores), mining, transportation, construction, and farming

Wyoming's economy is based on its natural resources, as well as revenue from agriculture and tourism.

and forestry. Finally about 5 percent of Wyomingites finding jobs in manufacturing.

In 2006 Wyoming ranked fifth in the United States in terms of creating new jobs. That is a great sign for the future of the state's economy.

Service industry jobs, such as tour guides, offer a wealth of employment opportunities in Wyoming.

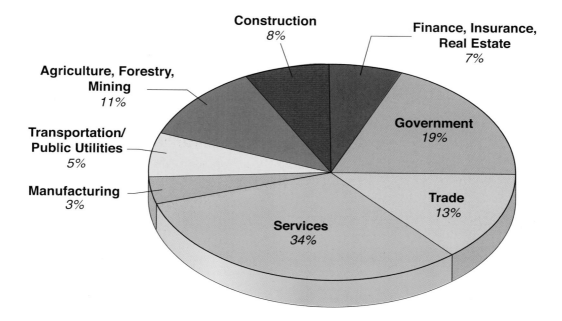

WYOMING WORKFORCE

Construction
8%

Finance, Insurance,
Real Estate
7%

Agriculture, Forestry,
Mining
11%

Transportation/
Public Utilities
5%

Manufacturing
3%

Government
19%

Trade
13%

Services
34%

AGRICULTURE

Traditionally, Wyoming has been an agricultural state. Although the number of ranches and farms in the state (currently around 9,200) has remained fairly steady, Wyoming's economy is not as dependent on farm and ranch products as it once was. Wyoming may be vast in land area, but its number of farms is small. This is mostly because the state receives little rainfall. Farms are mainly located in the eastern part of the state. There, crops like beans, sugar beets, and potatoes are grown. These farms also raise grain and hay to feed livestock. The most successful farms use irrigation systems to bring a steady supply of water to the crops.

Agriculture, though an important sector of Wyoming's economy, contributes only 2 percent to the gross state product.

What Wyoming lacks in farms it makes up for in ranches, which occupy 96 percent of the state's agricultural land. For some ranchers Wyoming's mythic cowboy lifestyle seems almost real. Thomas McNamee loves "the beautiful horses, the beautiful leather, the sun-crinkled squint toward the distant horizon." But, he adds, this life also involves "long hours, poor money, guaranteed uncertainty, and unending, brutally hard work." Few Wyoming ranches raise sheep today, but the beef industry is still strong, and the cowboy pictured on the Wyoming license plate remains a good symbol for the state's economy.

Despite the small number of farm and ranches, however, some of Wyoming's agricultural goods still lead the nation in production. For example, Wyoming ranks second in the production of wool and sheep, fifth in the cultivation of pinto beans, seventh in barley, ninth in sugar beets and all other dry beans, and twelfth in spring wheat. Cattle ranching still brings in the most money of all farm products, adding to the state's more than $1 billion yearly agricultural revenue.

A sheep wrangler rounds up his sheep for shearing.

THE ENERGY STATE

Although Wyoming has long been associated with cattle ranching, today energy is also an important industry, especially as the price of fuel continues to rise. Rigs for drilling oil and gas roar along roadsides across the state. Wyoming produces more coal than any other state. "We fill up eight or nine trains, each a mile long, every day," says Ken Miller of the Black Thunder coal mine in the Powder River Basin. Some of this coal fuels the giant Jim Bridger power plant near Rock Springs.

Black Thunder coal mine is one of the largest coal mines in the country.

2005 GROSS STATE PRODUCT: $27 Billion

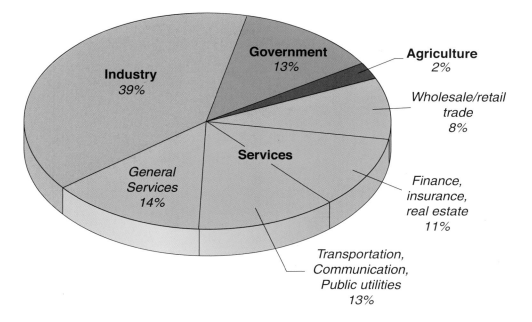

Industry
39%

Government
13%

Agriculture
2%

Wholesale/retail
trade
8%

Services

General
Services
14%

Finance,
insurance,
real estate
11%

Transportation,
Communication,
Public utilities
13%

The plant towers twenty-four stories above the sandy flatlands of the Great Divide Basin, which easily makes it the tallest building in Wyoming. It generates four times more electricity than Wyoming can use. Most of the rest is sold to other states.

The names of two other minerals mined in Wyoming are unknown to most Americans, even though people use them almost every day. One is trona (also called soda ash). Wyoming has almost the world's entire natural supply of trona at a single giant mine near the town of Green River. Trona is an ingredient in glass, paper, and baking soda, and is also used in making iron and steel.

The other unfamiliar mineral that is important to Wyoming's economy is bentonite—a fancy name for a fancy kind of mud. Bentonite can absorb fifteen times its volume in water and, when wet, it becomes so slippery that cars can barely drive over it. Wyoming is lucky to have large deposits of bentonite, which is used in making glue, paint, detergent, and polish, as well as makeup, toothpaste, and cat litter.

Other important energy sources include natural gas, Wyoming's most financially successful, and uranium, along with oil. In 2007 more than 400 million tons of coal were expected to be extracted from Wyoming's land, while about 18 million tons of trona were mined. More than three thousand new jobs were added to Wyoming's mining industry in 2006.

RELIEVING POVERTY

Even though many Wyomingites live comfortable lives, poverty, as stated in a 2006 report, affects over 10 percent of Wyoming's population. Most of Wyoming's poor are concentrated in small towns or in rural areas where there are few jobs. Due to poor employment outlets some of Wyoming's worst poverty was found on the Wind River Reservation. But there is now a good chance that the economy is changing there. As of 2007 there were three Native-American-owned gambling casinos in Wyoming, which had the potential to create $1 million in profit each year. Not only do the casinos provide jobs, but the profits also allow Native Americans to pay for better health care and to raise their standard of living. The casinos also attract tourists, which can help boost the entire state's revenue.

EARNING A LIVING

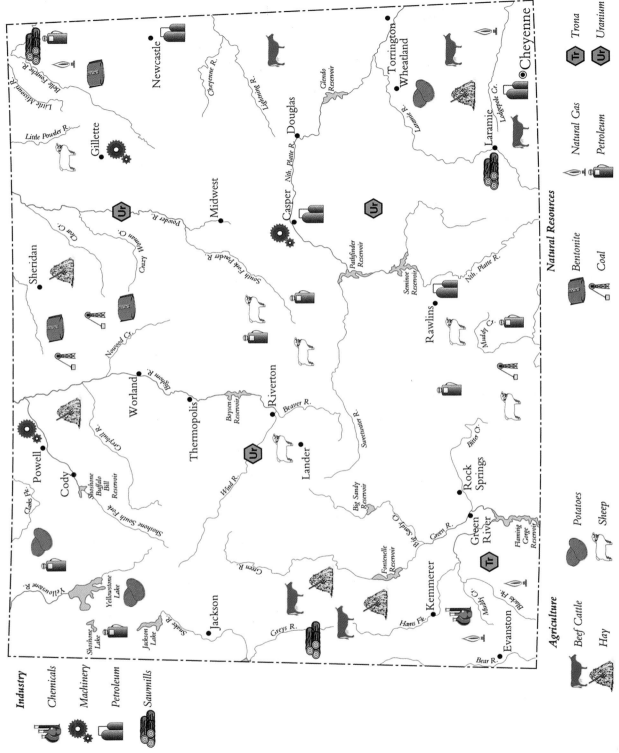

Newcastle

Cheyenne R.

Lightning R.

Glendo Reservoir

Torrington
Wheatland

Little Missouri R.

Belle Fourche R.

Little Powder R.

Gillette

Laramie R.

Lodgepole Cr.

Laramie

Douglas

Nth. Platte R.

Casper

Midwest

Powder R.

Clear Cr.

Crazy Woman Cr.

South Fork Powder R.

Pathfinder Reservoir

Seminoe Reservoir

Nth. Platte R.

Sheridan

Muddy Cr.

Rawlins

Nowood Cr.

Bighorn R.

Worland

Greybull R.

Thermopolis

Riverton

Beaver R.

Boysen Reservoir

Sweetwater R.

Lander

Bitter Cr.

Powell

Cody

Shoshone Buffalo Bill Reservoir

Clarks Fk.

Shoshone South Fork

Wind R.

Big Sandy Reservoir

Big Sandy Cr.

Rock Springs

Green R.

Green River

Flaming Gorge Reservoir

Yellowstone R.

Yellowstone Lake

Shoshone Lake

Jackson Lake

Snake R.

Jackson

Green R.

Greys R.

Fontenelle Reservoir

Kemmerer

Hams Fk.

Black's Fk.

Muddy Cr.

Evanston

Bear R.

Natural Resources

| | Bentonite | | Trona | Tr |
| Coal | | | Uranium | Ur |

Natural Gas

Petroleum

Agriculture

Beef Cattle

Hay

Potatoes

Sheep

Industry

Chemicals

Machinery

Petroleum

Sawmills

TOURISM

One of the brightest spots in today's economy is Wyoming's second-largest industry—tourism, which in 2007 provided jobs for more than 37,000 Wyomingites. About seven million people visit Wyoming every year. Wyoming's parks, such as Yellowstone and Grand Teton, as well as the state's overall natural beauty and abundant space, attract visitors from all over the world. Activities such as skiing, hunting, fishing, rock climbing, and pretending to be cowboys at dude ranches keep visitors coming and wanting more. Tourists bring revenue to the state by staying at hotels, eating at restaurants, buying gasoline for their vehicles, paying fees at campsites, and purchasing merchandise such as souvenirs, clothing, and equipment. There is a downside to tourism, however. Too many tourists

The second-most profitable industry in Wyoming is tourism.

can threaten wildlife and put pressure on the environment. So there is a need to monitor the benefits of tourist dollars against the need to keep Wyoming's natural surroundings healthy.

RESEARCH AND DEVELOPMENT

Wyoming's economy is at a crossroads, and state residents argue about which direction it should take. Some say Wyoming should continue to rely on mining. Others say Wyoming should build a mixed economy that can withstand the boom and bust of changing mineral prices, while also preserving the environment in order to attract tourists and new residents. Neither of these paths will be easy to travel, but Wyomingites' long tradition of hard work and self-reliance should help them meet their economic challenges.

One of the new directions that Wyomingites are pursuing is that of research and development, one of the major means of diversifying Wyoming's economy and attracting some of the best researchers to Wyoming. Toward this goal Wyoming is planning to create a $60 million data facility, developed by the National Center for Atmospheric Research (NCAR). The facility would house what is being referred to as a supercomputer, which may well be the most powerful computer in the world. Having access to this computer would mean that the University of Wyoming School of Energy Resources scientists and researchers could calculate and investigate innovative ways to mine and to use energy sources, among other things. The facility is projected to be completed in 2010.

As of 2007 Wyoming's economy was showing significant progress. It was one of the top states in new job creation and, with innovative ideas such as the NCAR supercomputer, Wyoming is demonstrating that diversification in the labor force is more than just a whimsical thought. Wyoming's economy is moving in a new direction, toward a positive destination.

Chapter Six

A Fantastic Voyage

Picture a box with a big letter *S* drawn inside it. The box is Wyoming, and the *S* is a route that tours the state. The box is not really a box; it is many different places and people. It is mountains and plains, towns and ranches, old settlements and new, and changing landscapes.

BLACK HILLS AND BIGHORNS

Beginning at the top of the *S*, in the upper right-hand corner of the state, we start in the Black Hills, a group of small mountains covered by dark pine forests. Most of the Black Hills are in South Dakota, but some extend into Wyoming. Dakotas and other Native Americans have long regarded the Black Hills as holy, including Devils Tower—a huge knuckle of fluted volcanic rock rising above the grasslands. Devils Tower is well known to those who have seen the movie *Close Encounters of the Third Kind* as the spot where an alien spaceship lands. Since that movie was made, more and more people have visited the tower, including many rock climbers who enjoy the challenge of scrambling up the channels in its surface.

A stop not to be missed on a visit to Wyoming is Grand Teton National Park.

Devils Tower, the remains of an ancient volcanic plug, stands 1,267 feet high.

Traveling west through the northern grasslands the dramatic Bighorn Mountains rise on the horizon. At their foot is Sheridan, a busy town that grew up around the cattle industry and still celebrates the ranching lifestyle with rodeos and cattle drives every summer. On its outskirts is the Eaton Ranch, one of the grandest of the old dude ranches, where droves of eastern tourists played cowboy in the early twentieth century. It's still open to guests. The Bighorns rise steeply from Sheridan—beautiful mountains of yellow and brown surrounding valleys dotted with flowers such as Indian paintbrush and wild rose.

THE STORY OF DEVILS TOWER

Here is a Dakota legend of how Devils Tower came to be.

After a long day of travel a Native-American tribe stopped on a riverbank. Seven small girls went off to play while their parents made camp. The girls wandered through the tall grasses, chasing each other farther and farther away from camp.

Suddenly they stumbled upon a slumbering bear. The bear awoke and began to chase them. The girls fled toward camp, but they could see that the bear was going to catch them. As they sprinted through the tall grass they came upon a big rock. They scrambled onto it and began to pray: "Oh, Rock, take pity on us!"

The rock heard the girls' pleas. It rose out of the ground, lifting them out of the bear's reach. The bear lunged again and again as the rock grew, breaking his claws as it tried to scramble toward the girls. The rock became a lofty tower, marked everywhere by the bear's scratches. The girls were pushed into the sky, where they became seven little stars—the ones that make up the constellation we now call the Pleiades. The bear stalked off through the grass and disappeared, but the tower remains.

Beyond the mountains the land flattens into Big Horn Basin, a dry expanse of sagebrush and sky. Near the town of Lovell is Wyoming's most important Indian artifact: the Medicine Wheel, a large circle of rocks on a high table of land with twenty-eight "spokes" radiating from its center. It is an ancient site, at least a thousand years old. Its purpose is a mystery, because the culture that built it disappeared long ago. Today's Indians have adopted it as a holy site and conduct religious ceremonies there.

Across the Big Horn Basin is the town of Cody, which is a monument to its founder, Buffalo Bill. Cody's western flavor and museums make it one of the most popular tourist destinations in Wyoming. The Buffalo Bill Museum is full of objects from Buffalo Bill's life, including firearms, cowboy gear, and souvenirs from the Wild West Show. The Plains Indian Museum features displays about many Native-American tribes, including art and artifacts of everyday life, such as tepees and weapons used for hunting bison. On the outskirts of Cody is Old Trail Town, a street lined with old houses and buildings that were rescued from around the state and moved here for display—including Butch Cassidy's cabin from the Hole-in-the-Wall.

Although Cheyenne disputes it, the town of Cody claims to be the Rodeo Capital of the World. The Cody Nite Rodeo takes place every evening during the summer, and kids' riding and roping events are a big part of the action. Cody also calls itself the Gateway to Yellowstone, and no one disputes that. The highway west of town wriggles through narrow Shoshone Canyon, cutting close to the roaring Shoshone River and disappearing into long, dark tunnels blasted through the cliffs that loom alongside it. Fifty miles from Cody the road reaches the east gate of Wyoming's greatest treasure.

The collection of buildings in Old Town date from 1879 to 1901.

The Shoshone River flows through the deep Shoshone Canyon.

YELLOWSTONE AND THE WESTERN MOUNTAINS

Created in 1872 Yellowstone is the nation's oldest national park, and its most popular. More than three million people visit the park every summer. The park contains some ten thousand "thermal features," from geysers that spew out water and steam to bubbling mudpots and boiling mineral springs. Old Faithful, which erupts almost every half hour, is the most famous. Most Yellowstone geysers erupt less frequently, but some of them are much more powerful. Giant Geyser shoots a plume of hot water skyward every ten days or so. Its eruptions last up to an hour and can eject a million gallons of

water. "It's really something you don't want to miss," says Ann Deutsch, a Yellowstone naturalist.

Another Yellowstone highlight is seeing the herds of bison and other wildlife, including grizzly bears and wolves. Adventurous types hike far into Yellowstone's forests and mountains, discovering sights that car-bound travelers can only imagine. In the winter, they ski or snowshoe to their destinations—most park roads close with the coming of snow. Some Yellowstone visitors camp, and others stay in hotels such as the Old Faithful Inn, the world's largest log building. During the summer many young people work at Yellowstone's hotels and campgrounds, or take jobs maintaining trails or serving as guides.

Every half hour, Old Faithful spouts hot water into the air that can reach 20 to 75 feet.

At Yellowstone it's common for visitors to see herds of bison crossing the road.

Passing south out of Yellowstone travelers arrive at the Teton Range. Grand Teton National Park is less developed than Yellowstone. It is a haven for hiking, horseback riding, and wildlife watching, as well as white-water rafting and fishing. The Tetons also attract thousands of mountain climbers every year. The snowcapped peaks stand alongside Jackson Hole, a spectacular valley containing Jackson and Jenny lakes. The town of Jackson has become a popular place for wealthy newcomers.

Jenny Lake, formed by melting glaciers, is one of the most beautiful lakes in the United States.

Heading back east from Jackson on the S-shaped tour is a giant roadblock, the Wind River Range. No road crosses it, so travelers must navigate around it. Surrounding the range is the Wind River Reservation, shared by the Shoshone and Arapaho Indians. This is a remote area, and few non-Indians visit it. Backpackers and mountain climbers see much more of this magnificent range and its glaciers, lakes, and meadows than car travelers do.

PLACES TO SEE

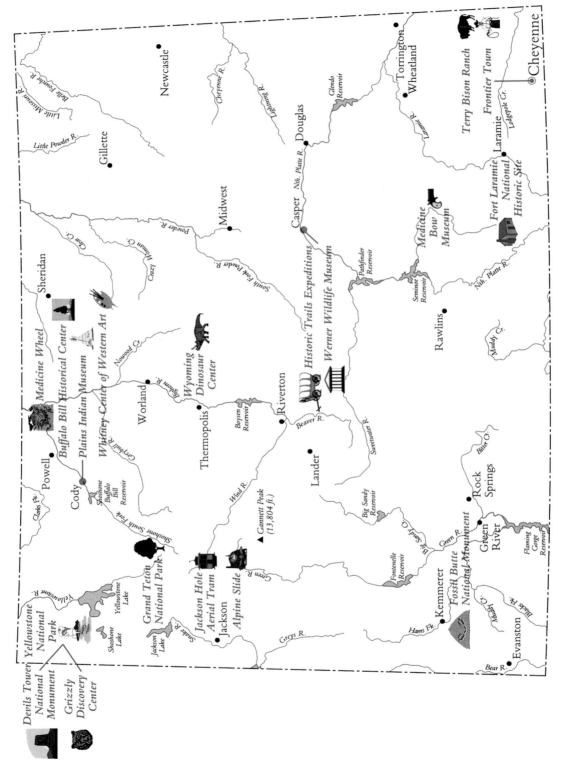

Newcastle

Torrington
Wheatland

Cheyenne

Gillette

Little Powder R.

Belle Fourche R.

Little Missouri R.

Cheyenne R.

Lightning R.

Glendo Reservoir

Nth. Platte R.

Douglas

Terry Bison Ranch

Frontier Town

Lodgepole Cr.

Midwest

Casper

Historic Trails Expeditions

Werner Wildlife Museum

Laramie R.

Medicine Bow Museum

Fort Laramie National Historic Site

Sheridan

Clear Cr.

Powder R.

South Fork Powder R.

Pathfinder Reservoir

Nth. Platte R.

Laramie

Medicine Wheel

Buffalo Bill Historical Center

Plains Indian Museum

Whitney Center of Western Art

Crazy Woman Cr.

Seminoe Reservoir

Rawlins

Muddy Cr.

Nowood Cr.

Wyoming Dinosaur Center

Bighorn R.

Riverton

Worland

Greybull R.

Thermopolis

Boysen Reservoir

Beaver R.

Sweetwater R.

Bitter Cr.

Powell

Cody

Shoshone Buffalo Bill Reservoir

Lander

Big Sandy Reservoir

Rock Springs

Green River

Clarks Fk.

Shoshone South Fork

Gannett Peak (13,804 ft.)

Wind R.

Big Sandy Cr.

Green R.

Fontenelle Reservoir

Flaming Gorge Reservoir

Yellowstone National Park

Yellowstone R.

Yellowstone Lake

Grand Teton National Park

Jackson Hole Aerial Tram

Alpine Slide

Green R.

Kemmerer

Fossil Butte National Monument

Shoshone Lake

Jackson Lake

Snake R.

Jackson

Greys R.

Hams Fk.

Muddy Cr.

Bear R.

Blacks Fk.

Evanston

Devils Tower National Monument

Grizzly Discovery Center

The reservation is dotted with very small settlements and a few towns. In one of them, Ethete, is Saint Michael's Mission, a circle of buildings that includes the striking Church of Our Father's House. The church is adorned with Native-American crafts and designs. Its altar is a large drum, and the window behind it looks out on the rising sun and the mountains.

The Wind River flows north out of the reservation and plunges through Wind River Canyon, another spectacular sight. The narrow cliffs are a thousand feet high on both sides of the churning river and cast deep shadows in the whole canyon when the sun is not directly overhead.

Nearby is the town of Thermopolis and its main attraction, Hot Springs State Park. The park contains the world's largest mineral hot springs, which discharge 4 million gallons of hot water every day from a multicolored pool banked by dripping mineral deposits. The water feeds a large outdoor swimming pool, which stays warm enough to attract bathers even during winter blizzards. It's a weird sight: bathing suits, cowboy hats, whirling snowflakes falling, and thick clouds of steam rising to meet them.

BACKWARD ALONG THE OREGON TRAIL

Heading east takes tourists and travelers out of the mountains and back onto the plains along a stretch of the Oregon Trail. There visitors can see Independence Rock and many other landmarks that guided the pioneers. At Martin's Cove, disaster struck a company of Mormons pushing handcarts toward Utah in late 1856. Snow, cold, disease, and hunger brought them to a halt there. A rescue team sent from Salt Lake City saved many lives, but at least a hundred died and were buried at Martin's Cove. "Please stay on the paths," signs read. "Many graves are unidentified."

THE MORMAN TRAIL REENACTMENT

In 1997 Mormons marked the 150th anniversary of their migration to Salt Lake City with a reenactment of the historic journey. Beginning in Omaha, Nebraska, a parade of wagons and handcarts followed the old trails across Nebraska and Wyoming to Utah. The three-month journey crossed a thousand miles of plains, mountains, and desert.

More than 150 Mormons, from small children to eighty-one-year-old Steve Ellis, participated in the reenactment. Oxen, horses, and mules pulled the wagons, but the dozens of handcarts that joined them were pulled by people, just as they were on the original trip. The wagon train spent six weeks crossing Wyoming, visiting historic sites along the way. At Fort Bridger, a newcomer joined the group when a baby, Henry Freestone Bentley, was born.

About six thousand Mormons died making this journey between 1847 and 1869. But many thousands more survived to build Salt Lake City and the state of Utah. Many of the people who took part in the reenactment were inspired by the hardships of their ancestors. "We've studied the pioneers," said one participant, "and the lessons they learned are ones I want my children to learn."

Casper, the first of the three so-called big cities on this tour of Wyoming, thrived during the oil boom of the 1970s and early 1980s, and it looks newly built compared to Wyoming's many Old West towns. From Casper visitors zoom south to the oldest settled corner of Wyoming. The speed limit on Wyoming's highways is 75 miles per hour, but it still takes more than two hours to reach Cheyenne. It takes even longer if one stops along the way—perhaps in Douglas, to see the town's giant statue of a jackelope (a mythical animal that has the body of a rabbit and the antlers of an antelope).

TEN LARGEST CITIES

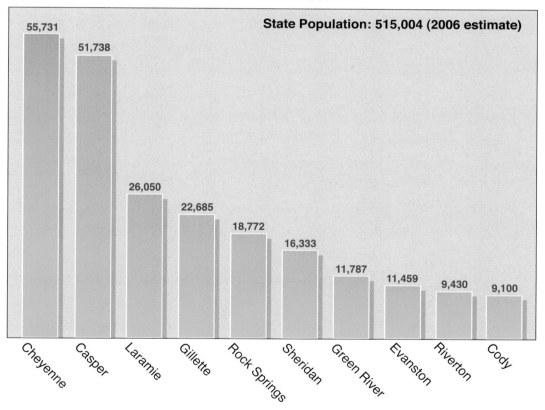

State Population: 515,004 (2006 estimate)

City	Population
Cheyenne	55,731
Casper	51,738
Laramie	26,050
Gillette	22,685
Rock Springs	18,772
Sheridan	16,333
Green River	11,787
Evanston	11,459
Riverton	9,430
Cody	9,100

Another tempting stop is Fort Laramie National Historic Site, which was built as a trading post in 1834 and became a military fort in 1849 to protect travelers on the Oregon Trail. The fort is the best-preserved relic of early settlement and military life in Wyoming. It has "the feeling of what it really must have been like then," says writer Nathaniel Burt. Many of the original buildings have been restored, including a two-story house called Old Bedlam, which housed rowdy soldiers. Built in 1849 it is the oldest building in the state.

ALONG THE UNION PACIFIC LINE

At Cheyenne travelers turn the final corner of the tour. Cheyenne was the first major city built as the Union Pacific Railroad began advancing across Wyoming in 1867. In the center of Cheyenne is Wyoming's capitol, which was finished just in time for statehood in 1890. Built of gray and tan stone, it looks solid and practical, like Wyoming—not like the gleaming white capitols in many other states.

Traveling west along the Union Pacific tracks takes visitors through the last mountain pass of this voyage, one of the windiest places in the United States. Sometimes Interstate 80, the freeway here, is closed for no other reason than the peril of whipping gusts. The wind has eroded the Vedauwoo rock formations between Cheyenne and Laramie into an eerie panorama of rounded, piled stones. They look like rolls of bread stacked in a bakery window.

Laramie, 49 miles west of Cheyenne, is the home of the University of Wyoming and its geological museum. Among its exhibits is the gigantic skeleton of an apatosaurus, a native of Wyoming's prehistoric swamps and the largest dinosaur ever discovered. Outside the museum stands a full-scale statue of *Tyrannosaurus rex*, the fiercest dinosaur ever to roam Wyoming—or anywhere else.

Rock climbers enjoy the wrinkles and rolls of the Vedauwoo rock formations.

On the Utah-Wyoming border is the Flaming Gorge National Recreation Area.

West of Laramie is Rawlins, the site of the Wyoming State Prison, a forbidding building that closed in 1982 and is now a museum. At night visitors feel their way through the prison on tours conducted in total darkness.

Rawlins is perched at the edge of the Red Desert and the Great Divide Basin. Very few people live there, but you are likely to see an abundance of wildlife, including some of the largest herds of pronghorn antelope and wild horses. On its western edge the steady wind has created the Killpecker Sand Dunes.

This corner of Wyoming is raw, dry, and flat—at least compared to other places in the state. Around the towns of Green River and Rock Springs are some of Wyoming's biggest mines, and even from the highway you can see the massive scale of these operations.

Just south of these towns is a fine place to relax and rest: Flaming Gorge. Carved by the Green River over millions of years the gorge was named for its brilliantly colored rock and the sculpted land surrounding it. Once the Green River roared through the gorge, but now it is a huge reservoir, thanks to a controversial dam in Utah. The dam transformed the steep-walled river canyon into a 90-mile-long lake. Though many Wyomingites regret the loss of that unique landscape, others flock to the new Flaming Gorge with speedboats and fishing tackle, for it is an angler's hot spot filled with trout and other fish. Even though much of its former glory is now underwater, it is still one of the most beautiful places in Wyoming—and perhaps the world.

Now you have drawn your *S,* a long voyage that may be taken by car, train, bicycle, horse, snowshoes, or airplane. We have only imagined the journey. Start planning now for the real thing!

THE FLAG: *Adopted in 1917 the state flag depicts a buffalo with the state seal "branded" on its side. The blue background has two borders: white, symbolizing purity, and red, standing for the Native Americans and the blood of the pioneers.*

THE SEAL: *The state seal, adopted in 1893, shows a woman and the motto "Equal Rights." They symbolize Wyoming's early commitment to civil rights for women. A cowboy and a miner stand next to the woman, representing the state's two important industries: livestock and mining.*

State Survey

Statehood: July 10, 1890

Origin of Name: From the Algonquin Indian phrase *Maugh-wau-wa-ma*, meaning "large plains," or from the Delaware Indian phrase for "mountains and valleys alternating."

Nicknames: The Equality State, The Cowboy State

Capital: Cheyenne

Motto: Equal Rights

Bird: Meadowlark

Flower: Indian paintbrush

Tree: Plains Cottonwood

Gem: Jade

Fish: Cutthroat trout

Mammal: Bison

Reptile: Horned toad

Fossil: Knightia

Dinosaur: Triceratops

Meadowlark

Indian paintbrush

WYOMING MARCH SONG

In the summer of 1903 Judge Charles E. Winter of Casper wrote a poem entitled "Wyoming." It wasn't until the 1920s that George E. Knapp, the director of the music department of the University of Wyoming at Laramie, set the poem to music. Another thirty years passed before the "Wyoming March Song" was adopted as the official state song in 1955.

Words by Charles E. Winter   **Music by George E. Knapp**

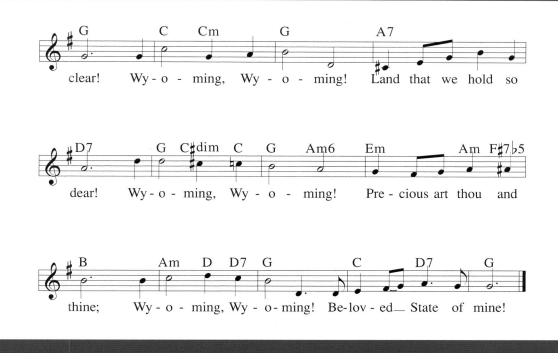

GEOGRAPHY

Highest point: 13,804 feet above sea level at Gannett Peak

Lowest point: 3,100 feet above sea level at Belle Fourche River in Crook County

Area: 97,914 square miles

Greatest Distance North to South: 276 miles

Greatest Distance East to West: 364 miles

Bordering States: Montana to the north and west, South Dakota and Nebraska to the east, Colorado to the south, Utah to the south and west, Idaho to the west

Hottest Recorded Temperature: 114° F at Basin on July 12, 1900

Coldest Recorded Temperature: –66° F at Moran on February 9, 1933

Average Annual Precipitation: 14.5 inches

Major Rivers: Bighorn, Green, North Platte, Powder, Snake, Yellowstone

Major Lakes: Bighorn, Flaming Gorge, Pathfinder, Saratoga, Yellowstone

Trees: aspen, cottonwood, Douglas fir, Engelmann spruce, lodgepole pine, ponderosa pine, subalpine fir

Wild Plants: arnica, bluegrass, buttercup, cactus, evening star, five-finger, flax, forget-me-not, goldenrod, redtop, sagebrush, saxifrage, sour dock, tufted fescue, wheat grass, windflower

Animals: black-footed ferret, beaver, black bear, coyote, elk, fox, grizzly bear, lynx, marten, moose, mountain lion, mule deer, pronghorn, raccoon, otter, white-tailed deer, whooping crane, Wyoming toad

Birds: bald eagle, duck, golden eagle, goose, grouse, pheasant, sage hen, wild turkey

Fish: bass, bluegill, channel catfish, crappie, sauger, ling, trout, walleye

Endangered Animals: black-footed ferret, Colorado pikeminnow, gray wolf, Kendall Warm Springs dace, razorback sucker, whooping crane, Wyoming toad

Endangered Plants: butterfly plant, blowout penstemon, Ute ladies' tresses, and desert yellowhead

Black-footed ferret

TIMELINE

10,000 B.C.E. The Clovis people are one of the earliest groups to live in the area of present-day Wyoming.

8,000 B.C.E. The Folsom people arrive in what is now Wyoming.

6,000 B.C.E. The Eden Valley people hunt on the land of present-day Wyoming.

1500 C.E. Shoshone, Arapaho, Lakota, Crow, Cheyenne, Bannock, and Northern Ute live in the region.

1742 François Louis Verendrye may have been the first explorer to enter the area of present-day Wyoming.

1807 John Colter explores the Yellowstone area.

1812 Robert Stuart discovers South Pass as a route through the Rocky Mountains.

1832 First wagons travel the Oregon Trail through South Pass, opening the West to settlers.

1834 William Sublette and Robert Campbell establish Fort William (later renamed Fort Laramie), the first permanent trading post in Wyoming.

1843 Fort Bridger, Wyoming's second permanent settlement, is established.

1849 U.S. government buys Fort Laramie.

1852 First school in Wyoming is opened at Fort Laramie by William Vaux and his daughter, Victoria.

1860s Tension along the Powder River erupts into fighting between settlers and Native Americans.

1863 Wyoming's first newspaper, *The Daily Telegraph*, is published at Fort Bridger.

1866 Chief Red Cloud and Lakota surprise a U.S. cavalry group, killing all eighty-one soldiers.

1867 Union Pacific Railroad enters Wyoming; Cheyenne is founded.

1869 Wyoming legislature gives women the right to vote and hold office.

1870 Esther Morris becomes the first female justice of the peace in the United States.

1872 Yellowstone becomes the world's first national park.

1876 War breaks out between the United States and Native-American tribes as thousands of settlers invade the lands in search of gold; U.S. troops destroy a Cheyenne camp along the Powder River, leaving Native Americans to freeze or starve to death.

1883 First oil well is drilled in Wyoming.

1887 The University of Wyoming opens in Laramie.

1888 The capitol is completed in Cheyenne.

1890 Wyoming becomes the forty-fourth state.

1892 A cattle rustling dispute between large cattle ranchers and smaller ranchers erupts into the Johnson County War.

1900 Chief Washakie is buried with full military honors at Fort Washakie.

1906 Devils Tower becomes the first national monument.

1918 Uranium is discovered near Lusk.

1925 Nellie Tayloe Ross becomes Wyoming's governor, the first female governor in United States.

1929 Grand Teton National Park opens.

1951–1952 Major uranium deposits are discovered in many parts of state.

1958 Nation's first operational intercontinental ballistic missile base opens near Cheyenne.

1978 Largest radio telescope in the world is built on Jelm Mountain.

1988 Fire damages more than 1 million acres in Yellowstone National Park.

1989 Wyomingite Richard "Dick" Cheney becomes the U.S. secretary of defense.

1995 Wolves taken from Canada are reintroduced in Wyoming at Yellowstone National Park.

2001 Dick Cheney becomes vice president of the United States.

2003 David Freudenthal is voted in as Wyoming's thirty-first governor, and twelfth Democratic governor.

2006 First of Wyoming high school seniors qualify for the Hathaway Scholarship.

2007 Debate continues in legislature about the delisting of wolves from endangered status in Wyoming.

ECONOMY

Agricultural Products: beef cattle, corn, dairy products, sheep, sugar beets, wheat

Manufactured Products: chemicals, glass and clay products, lumber and wood products, petroleum products

Natural Resources: bentonite, coal, iron ore, natural gas, petroleum, stone, trona

Business and Trade: tourism, transportation, utilities

Cattle

CALENDAR OF CELEBRATIONS

Wyoming State Winter Fair Lander breaks up Wyoming's long, brutal winter with a celebration early in each new year. Highlights include horse, cat, dog, and even llama shows. The musical entertainment, food, and fun take the chill off.

International Rocky Mountain Stage Stop Sled Dog Race In early winter a 400-mile dogsled race winds through nine Wyoming counties. Each night the teams stop in a different town, which greets the hearty human and canine racers with food and enthusiasm.

Days of '49 During the second weekend of June, Greybull hosts its "Boots, Hooves, and Wheels Rodeo," featuring a traditional rodeo, parades, demolition derby, and other family events. Why is it called Days of '49? The Greybull Jaycees first held this big weekend event in 1949.

Bozeman Trail Days The cavalry rides again for three days every June when Story celebrates one hundred years of Wyoming history. Retrace the dangerous route of gold-seeking settlers who took a shortcut through Indian lands. Watch colorful cavalry exhibitions and Native American dancing.

Mustang Days Modern-day cowboys and cowgirls rope steers and ride bucking broncos and angry bulls at this classic rodeo in Lovell during the last week in June. The event also includes a chuckwagon breakfast, parades, street dancing, a family fun festival, a demolition derby, a barbecue, and fireworks to top it all off.

Ten Sleep Rodeo Days For the past fifty years the Fourth of July in Ten Sleep has been rodeo time. When the sun sets, tourists, rodeo riders, and townspeople enjoy an old-fashioned street dance.

Sheepherder's Rodeo Each July Kaycee proves you *can* have a rodeo without cattle. This sheep rodeo features sheep-roping, sheep-riding, and sheep-hooking. You can also watch sheepdogs at work—responding only to signals from their owners, they separate and pen a designated number of sleep.

Pioneer Days During the third week of July the people of Cowley celebrate their pioneer heritage with parades, dancing, a rodeo, and other contests. This event has also become a traditional time for family and school reunions in Cowley.

Cheyenne Frontier Days If you can't get enough of rodeo excitement come to Cheyenne's Frontier Days in July for a week of roping, bucking, and riding. Each day after the rodeo ends the famous Frontier Days Wild House Race pits teams of amateur cowboys against young, unbroken broncos. Parades during the week

Cheyenne Frontier Days

feature the world's largest collection of horse-drawn vehicles, along with antique carriages, floats, marching bands, clowns, and drill teams. You can also get a free breakfast of flapjacks and ham during the event. In 1996, 39,111 people ate free in one day! The midway offers carnival rides, games, entertainment, and food.

Dayton Days At the end of July Dayton hosts three days of fun, including a parade, Indian dancing, contests, street entertainment and dances, and food and craft booths. On the last day the town sponsors a hamburger feed.

Washakie County Fair In August Worland hosts a humdinger of a county fair, complete with 4-H livestock exhibits, homegrown crops, and cooking contests—and that's just for starters. Big-name country singers such as Reba McEntire perform at this fair, and you'll also enjoy the classic car show and a great rodeo.

Johnson County Fair and Rodeo The activities of the 4-H clubs take center stage at this county fair in Buffalo each August. A favorite contest features children and sheep dressed in coordinating costumes. Both youth and local ranchers compete in rodeos. The parade includes a fascinating assortment of horses, buggies, pack animals, floats, and people in costume.

Bighorn Mountain Polka Days You'll have a hard time standing still when you hear the lively music of great polka bands. Polka dancers from more than twenty-five states and Canada come to Sheridan for the three-day Labor Day weekend to celebrate this dance.

Harvest Festival Worland celebrates its farming heritage early in September with a pie-eating contest, beet carving, food booths, crafts, and street dancing. It's a friendly, small-town carnival.

STATE STARS

James Bridger (1804–1881) was one of the West's most famous mountain men. Born in Virginia, he moved to Illinois when he was eight. As a teen he took part in a trapping expedition. He and four partners later bought the Rocky Mountain Fur Company. Between 1838 and 1843, he planned and built Fort Bridger, which became an important trading post, military post, and Pony Express station. He also served as a guide on several expeditions. Bridger is also believed to have been the first white person to visit the Great Salt Lake.

Richard "Dick" Cheney (1941–) was U.S. secretary of defense from 1989 to 1993 under President George H. W. Bush. He also held an advisory position in Richard Nixon's administration and was chief of staff to President Gerald Ford. Cheney served five terms as a U.S. representative from Wyoming and was a staunch advocate of strengthening national defense. In 2000 he was chosen by George W. Bush to become the vice president of the United States.

Richard "Dick" Cheyney

John Colter (1775–1813), born in Virginia, was a fur trader and guide. In 1807 he explored the area that is now Yellowstone National Park and was the first to return east with tales of the region's steaming geysers. Before that journey, he had taken part in the Lewis and Clark expedition.

June Etta Downey (1875–1932), born in Laramie, was a psychologist and author. She attended and taught at the University of Wyoming. Downey was a pioneer in the study of personality, and she also researched imagination and creativity, color blindness, and handwriting. She wrote many books about her research, as well as works of poetry.

Curt Gowdy (1919–2006), a sportscaster, was born in Green River and graduated from the University of Wyoming. In 1943 he began his career as a sportswriter and local radio broadcaster. From 1951 to 1965, he was the voice of the Boston Red Sox. He went on to cover National Football League games, the Super Bowl, the World Series, and many other sporting events on NBC. He also hosted ABC's *Wide World of Sports* and *American Sportsman*. Gowdy was named to the Sports Broadcasters' Hall of Fame in 1981.

Jacques Laramie (1785?–1821), a trapper, was probably born in Canada. In 1819 he traveled to the unexplored southeastern part of Wyoming. He is believed to be the first white person to see the upper portion of the river that is named for him.

Esther Morris (1814–1902), born in New York, settled in Wyoming Territory in 1869. She is called the mother of women's suffrage because she was active in helping women obtain the right to vote in other states. She was, after all, from Wyoming—the first place in the United States where women won that right. In 1870 she became the first female justice of the peace in the United States.

Bill Nye (1850–1896) was a journalist and an important American humorist in the late nineteenth century. He was born in Maine and moved to Wisconsin as a child. He settled in Laramie in 1876 and began contributing to the *Denver Tribune* and the *Cheyenne Sun*. His humor in the *Laramie Boomerang*, which he helped found in 1881, was widely reprinted. His collections of columns were published in several books, including *Bill Nye and Boomerang* and *Bill Nye's History of the U.S.*

James Cash Penney (1870–1971) founded the J. C. Penney chain of department stores. He was born in Missouri, and in 1897 moved to Colorado, where he worked in a dry goods store. In 1902 he was sent to Kemmerer, Wyoming, to open a second store. He invested in the store and soon bought out his partners. Later he bought the store from his employees.

Jackson Pollock

Jackson Pollock (1912–1956), an important American artist, was born in Cody, Wyoming. Pollock moved to New York City in 1929 to study art. He developed his own innovative techniques and style, pouring, dripping, and flinging paint onto his canvases. Pollock's paintings, masterpieces of abstract impressionism, transformed American art.

Nellie Taylor Ross (1876–1977) became the nation's first woman governor in 1925 when she was elected to finish her deceased husband's term as governor of Wyoming. In 1933 President Franklin D. Roosevelt named Ross the first female director of the U.S. Mint. During her tenure, the Roosevelt dime and Jefferson nickel were introduced. She was born in Missouri.

Nellie Taylor Ross

Alan K. Simpson (1931–   ), a Republican senator, was born in Colorado and grew up in Cody. His father, Milward, was governor of Wyoming from 1955 to 1959. Simpson received his undergraduate and law degrees from the University of Wyoming. He served in the state legislature from 1965 to 1977 and was elected to the U.S. Senate in 1978. As a senator he was a leading voice in immigration reform.

Jedediah Strong Smith (1799–1831), born in New York, was a fur trader and explorer. He discovered the South Pass through the Rocky Mountains, a gateway to the Far West. He also opened the overland route to California through the Great Basin and the Sierra Nevadas and the overland trail from California to the Columbia River.

Spotted Tail (1833–1881), a Lakota chief, was born near Fort Laramie. He urged compromise to avoid violence with American settlers and was a key player in his nephew Crazy Horse's surrender to the United States in 1877. Nevertheless the Lakota were driven from their land. Spotted Tail was shot by one of his own people in 1881 for political reasons.

Spotted Tail

Francis Emroy Warren (1844–1929) was called the Dean of U.S. Senators because of the thirty-seven years he served in the Senate. He was born in Massachusetts and fought in the Civil War, earning a Congressional Medal of Honor. He migrated west and was appointed governor of Wyoming Territory in 1885. In 1890 he was elected the first governor of the new state of Wyoming, but he left that office soon after to become a U.S. senator. By the end of his time in office he had become the last Union soldier still serving in Congress.

Washakie (1804?–1900), probably born in Idaho or Utah, was a Shoshone chief in southwest Wyoming. He is famous for his diplomacy and for helping white settlers. He also acted as a U.S. Army guide for twenty years. Because of his diplomatic skill his tribe's experience with settlers and the U.S. government was less violent than that of many other tribes.

TOUR THE STATE

Yellowstone National Park In 1872 Yellowstone became the world's first national park. It is known the world over for its hot springs and geysers, including the most famous one, Old Faithful, which releases steam and enormous bursts of scalding water high into the air. Wildlife, such as grizzlies, black bears, elk, moose, and bighorn sheep, thrive in this park. Be sure to visit the Grand Canyon of the Yellowstone, which is noted for its dramatic colors, and the Paintpots, large springs filled with hot clay ranging in color from white to pink to black.

Buffalo Bill Historical Center (Cody) This complex includes four museums: The Buffalo Bill Museum displays items owned by showman and Pony Express rider Buffalo Bill. The Cody Firearms Museum traces the history of firearms. The Plains Indian Museum includes a large collection of ceremonial artifacts and weapons. And the Whitney Gallery of Western Art contains paintings and sculptures by famous artists such as George Catlin and Frederic Remington.

Old Trail Town (Cody) Historic buildings, such as the log cabin hideout of Butch Cassidy and the Sundance Kid, have been moved to this site from throughout the state. You will also find the grave of mountain man John "Jeremiah" Johnson here.

Wyoming Dinosaur Center (Thermopolis) If you love dinosaurs, this center is for you. On display are the remains of real dinosaurs, including the skeletons of triceratops—the state's official dinosaur—and a large sauropod. You can view preparation rooms to see what goes on behind the scenes of a working museum. You can also visit dig sites where crews are still uncovering dinosaur bones, talk to the crew, and even try your hand at digging up part of a dinosaur.

National Bighorn Sheep Interpretive Center (Dubois) Learn about bighorn sheep through dioramas, videos, and Sheep Mountain, a model of the animals' habitat.

Sheridan Inn (Sheridan) Built in 1892 historic Sheridan Inn was once considered the finest hotel between Chicago and San Francisco. Buffalo Bill was part-owner of this grand old building from 1894 to 1902 and auditioned acts for his world-renowned Wild West Show from the front porch. It was named a National Historic Landmark in 1965.

Jim Gatchell Museum of the West (Buffalo) This regional history museum is located at the foot of the Bighorn Mountains. Jim Gatchell was a frontier pharmacist who opened a drugstore in Buffalo in 1900. The Jim Gatchell Museum features a large collection of Indian artifacts. It also houses rare, frontier-era photographs of Wyoming, as well as artifacts, tools, and weapons from nearby forts.

Devils Tower National Monument (Sundance) This unusual geological formation has sides that shoot straight up 867 feet into the air and a flat top with sagebrush and grass growing on it. You can camp, hike, or picnic nearby, or visit the prairie dog colony near the entrance. The monument was featured in the movie *Close Encounters of the Third Kind*.

Hell's Half Acre (Powder River) This area is sometimes called the Baby Grand Canyon because of its bright rocks and geological formations. The canyon is filled with great stone towers and spires.

Homesteaders Museum (Torrington) This collection of pioneer artifacts is located in a former Union Pacific Railroad depot. The museum's displays illustrate what homestead life was like from the 1880s to the 1920s.

Fort Laramie National Historic Site (Fort Laramie) Eleven buildings of this nineteenth-century fort have been restored, including the cavalry barracks, which housed federal troops stationed to protect settlers on their way west. During the summer costumed guides give visitors a taste of daily military and civilian life on the post.

Fort Laramie National Historic Site

Cheyenne Frontier Days Old West Museum (Cheyenne) Horse-drawn wagons and other vehicles are on display here. You can also try out your rodeo skills on a mechanical bucking saddle.

Wyoming Territorial Prison and Old West Park (Laramie) Butch Cassidy and other famous outlaws once called this prison home. You can also watch actors re-create the historic trial in which women served on a jury for the first time.

Independence Rock State Historic Site (Alcova) More than five thousand explorers, adventurers, and soldiers carved their names on this well-known landmark along the Oregon Trail.

Fossil Butte National Monument (Kemmerer) Take a hike to one of the richest fossil beds in the world, where you will find traces of freshwater fish that swam there more than fifty million years ago. Before setting out on your hike you can get a close-up look at the fossils of mammals, plants, and fish at the visitors center.

Teton Country Wagon Train (Jackson Hole) You may have a new appreciation for cars after spending four days and three nights on a wagon-train trip along the roads between Grand Teton and Yellowstone national parks. Every night you will make camp at a new spot and settle in for dinner and song. The next day, before breaking camp, you can take canoe and horseback excursions into the countryside.

Grand Teton National Park (Jackson) This park is 485 square miles of magnificent mountainous wilderness. Lakes, glaciers, snowfields, and forests are waiting to be explored. Choose your transportation—horse, wagon, raft, canoe, or your own feet.

FUN FACTS

In 1902 Buffalo Bill Cody opened the luxurious Irma Hotel in Cody for visitors to Yellowstone. The two-story building cost $80,000. He invited governors, ranchers, military officers, scouts, sheepherders, and other frontier people to the opening. The hundreds of guests were treated to a meal never before seen in Wyoming—scalloped oysters, shrimp and tomato salads, roast turkey, boiled ham, sliced tongue, spring chicken, fresh fruit, sugared dates, nuts, cakes, and raspberry and pineapple sherbet. He even hired an orchestra from Lincoln, Nebraska, and his guests danced until dawn.

Grand Teton National Park

Many place names in Wyoming have interesting origins. The name Hell's Half Acre suggests something small, but it is actually a 320-acre area filled with unusual formations. Hell's Half Acre was once known as Devils Kitchen. According to one story the name change was the result of a mistake by a printer. Merchants wanted to attract more tourists, so they had professional pictures taken and set them to be printed as postcards. The printer titled the image Hell's Half Acre, but the merchants used the postcards anyway. Ten Sleep gets its name from the Native-Americans' measure of distance by the number of "sleeps" between locations. Ten Sleep was ten sleeps from a main winter camp.

The largest coal mine in the United States is Black Thunder, located near Wright, Wyoming.

There are two U.S. submarines named for Wyoming: the U.S.S. *Wyoming* and the U.S.S. *Cheyenne.*

The first person to ski down the 13,772-foot-high Grand Teton peak was Jackson Hole, Wyoming, resident Bill Briggs. He accomplished this feat in 1971.

Dinosaur footprints that are estimated to be 165 million years old were found near Shell, Wyoming, in 1997.

Find Out More

There are lots of interesting books about Wyoming, and many ways to explore the state on the World Wide Web. Here are a few to try first.

BOOKS

State Books

Dougherty, Michael. *Ultimate Wyoming Atlas and Travel Encyclopedia.* Bozeman, MT: Ultimate Press, 2003.

Hanson-Harding, Alexandra. *Wyoming.* Danbury, CT: Children's Press, 2003.

McCoy, Michael. *Wyoming Off the Beaten Path.* Guilford, CT: Globe Pequot, 2003.

Rea, Tom. *Devil's Gate: Owning the Land, Owning the Story.* Norman: University of Oklahoma Press, 2006.

SPECIAL INTEREST BOOKS

Ducher, Jim, and Helen Cherullo, James Manfull. *Living with Wolves.* Seattle: Mountaineers Books, 2005.

Halfpenny, James C. *Yellowstone's Wolves in the Wild.* Helena, MT: Riverbend Publishing, 2003.

Hawley, Russell J. *Fossil Critters of Wyoming*. Casper, WY: Endeavor Books, 2006.

Sutter, Virginia J. *Tell Me, Grandmother: Traditions, Stories, and Cultures of Arapaho People*. Boulder: University Press of Colorado, 2004.

WEB SITES

Yellowstone National Park
http///www.nps.gov.yell/
This is the official Yellowstone National Park site. You can check out the webcams or read about things to do in the park.

Wyoming Tales and Trails
http///www.wyomingtalesandtrails.com/
Find old photographs and history of Wyoming. There is even some cowboy music at this site.

Eastern Shoshone Tribe
http///www.easternshoshone.net/
Information about the Wind River Reservation, home of Shoshone and Arapaho people, is found here.

Index

Page numbers in **boldface** are illustrations and charts.

ABOUT THE AUTHORS

Guy Baldwin is a writer in New York City and a frequent visitor to Wyoming. He has climbed Devils Tower in the Wind River Mountains and hiked in the Tetons and the Bighorns. His favorite Wyoming memories are of its people, who are keepers of a rare treasure.

Joyce Hart is a freelance writer who has crossed the United States along back roads many times. In her travels she has driven through Wyoming, east to west and north to south, enjoying the wide open expanse of land and all the natural beauty. Currently she lives in Washington, another state that also enjoys a wealth of mountains and wildlife.